GURGAON
TO
GURUGRAM

Suptendu P. Biswas is an urban theorist, who works on the overlapping fields of design & planning in areas of built environment, spatial equity, landscape urbanism, urban heritage and socio-cultural studies. An architect, urban designer and planning professional, he has been involved in consultancy, teaching, research and writing for almost three decades. His multi-faceted works have been presented, published and exhibited in India and abroad.

A recipient of Senior Fellowship from the Ministry of Culture, Government of India, Dr Biswas is also one of the partners of VSPB Associates, an international award-winning architecture, urban design and landscape firm in New Delhi, a visiting faculty member of post-graduate courses at the School of Planning and Architecture (SPA), New Delhi, and one of the founder trustees of SEARCH, a Kolkata-based charitable trust working on urban sustainability and related spheres. He graduated from B.E. College (IIEST), Shibpur, and did his post-graduation and doctorate from SPA.

His first book, *Assorted City* (2015), was critically acclaimed and nominated among top five urban writings. He also co-edited *Blue Lines of Kolkata* (2017), a book on ideas and proposals about the canals of Kolkata. Dr Biswas is a keen observer of politics and urbanity and its inter-relationships.

GURGAON TO GURUGRAM
A Short Biography

SUPTENDU P. BISWAS

Published by
Rupa Publications India Pvt. Ltd 2021
7/16, Ansari Road, Daryaganj
New Delhi 110002

Sales centres:
Allahabad Bengaluru Chennai
Hyderabad Jaipur Kathmandu
Kolkata Mumbai

Copyright © Suptendu P. Biswas 2021

The views and opinions expressed in this book are the author's own and the facts are as reported by him which have been verified to the extent possible, and the publishers are not in any way liable for the same.

All rights reserved.
No part of this publication may be reproduced, transmitted, or stored in a retrieval system, in any form or by any means, electronic, mechanical, photocopying, recording or otherwise, without the prior permission of the publisher.

ISBN: 978-93-90356-40-9

First impression 2021

10 9 8 7 6 5 4 3 2 1

The moral right of the author has been asserted.

Printed at Saurabh Printers Pvt. Ltd, Noida

This book is sold subject to the condition that it shall not, by way of trade or otherwise, be lent, resold, hired out, or otherwise circulated, without the publisher's prior consent, in any form of binding or cover other than that in which it is published.

CONTENTS

Preface / *vii*

Transition / 1

Ambition / 40

Impression / 64

Contradiction / 90

Reflection / 124

Postscript / 145

Acknowledgements / 147

Notes / 149

PREFACE

Gurgaon was renamed Gurugram in 2016. The new name was inspired by the mythological epic Mahabharata, in which the village was donated as gurudakshina to Guru Dronacharya by the Pandavas. In this book, I refer to the city as Gurgaon only because a major part of the biographical narrative that I have tried to present precedes its newly acquired name.

Can contemporary Gurgaon ever be overtaken by the mythology surrounding it? I do not have the answer to that question, and in fact, I do not recall encountering such a question during my engagement with the city. Talking about Gurgaon poses a dilemma to me: should I explain it with maps and data like a research project, or should I only use anecdotal evidence to build a story? In the course of working with the city for over a decade, I have come across many incidents and had discussions on multiple urban aspects. I have used only a few of those, in order to weave a broader generic narrative.

Gurgaon began with the transition of land: from an agricultural asset to the real estate dividend. A new set of people started settling in Gurgaon, who had the ambition of having their own house on a plot of land. A unique urban imagery was created that portrayed the attractive, global and aspirational impression of the city. As more and more people came into Gurgaon for work, the city became a place for professionals and the educated class. Following them, support personnel flocked into the city in search of livelihood. The place also witnessed widespread demographic changes in its erstwhile villages. Like many other cities in India, Gurgaon, too, has been facing its own contradictions.

Each city lives in sets of layers and Gurgaon is no exception. The transition from Gurgaon to Gurugram represents one such set of layers that I intend to explore and reflect upon.

TRANSITION

From Agriculture to Urban

'*Mera pota hai, saab.*' (He is my grandson.) I overheard an old man telling a bank officer. He was possibly in his late 70s, dressed in typical Haryanvi attire—white kurta, dhoti and big white pagri (turban). He was accompanied by a schoolboy who, I assumed, was his grandson. No one could miss the well-oiled long stick that the man was holding. One of my colleagues had told me that such sticks are colloquially known as 'lath', from the vernacular word 'lathi'. He was also carrying an ordinary-looking thaila, a cotton bag.

This was sometime in 2004. We were at an extension counter of a bank in Gurgaon where the old man had come to deposit money. After a while, he opened his not-so-impressive bag and it was full of cash. He was like a magician, I felt! He did not know how to count so much money, so his grandson helped him. Perhaps, the boy had been brought along for that purpose: a school-going member of the family could give the moral support needed during such transactions. One could figure out that the man had sold his land and was depositing a part of the money received.

This is a symptomatic story of urban expansion in which land connects many latent dots. Urbanization starts with land and any change in the configuration of land effects an alteration in urban morphology. The story of Gurgaon is about its land and its possible modifications, from alteration of land use to that of ownership. Land changes hands in Gurgaon very often and the change in ownership leads to the consolidation and amalgamation of land parcels, coalesced to form different configurations. In fact, during the course of a semester with architecture students, we found that the land-ownership map of an area along Golf Course Road had swapped twice, thus reshaping the land configuration. This has been a continuous process of the making of Gurgaon.

∽

Gurgaon, to me, is an outcome of the manipulation of the gaps in planning and policy framework; the city is built around policy fault lines. In turn, this had led to certain weaknesses, which have been reversed to create opportunities. The city has been put together by an underlying politics and not by the holistic ambition of planning. Sometimes, we make the mistake of judging Gurgaon through the lens of comprehensive planning, which was not at all the starting point here. It is an example of what I call 'assorted city', piecemeal urban expansion without any pretension of attaining any sort of similarities or relationships between such pieces. In fact, Gurgaon is built out of imagined differences—how one building, plot or enclave can be made different from others, especially from the next-door neighbour. One can criticize such a process of city-making, but one must also accept at the same time that Gurgaon also exposes the limitations of conventional text-based building bylaws in instilling some sort of urban continuity.

Since the 1970s, Gurgaon's land situation has been poised curiously within a certain legal and planning framework. The 'Delhi Master Plan 1962' identified Gurgaon as a part of its inherent mega-ambition of creating a Regional Plan. The concept of a National Capital Region (NCR) was floated. Later, the NCR Plan too envisaged Gurgaon as a satellite in its hub-spoke model. However, the underlying process behind the current city's existence had been initiated since independence by a series of apparently autonomous, but ideologically connected policy decisions.

The Planning Commission initially focussed a lot on the irrigation system to reap agricultural dividends. Just after independence, a large section, about 72 per cent, of India's working population were engaged in the agrarian sector. Hence, schemes for the improvement of agriculture were relevant in Gurgaon district which, as part of Punjab at that time, was one of the beneficiaries of the Green Revolution. However, a low water table, lack of fertile land and absence of a major river in the vicinity were limitations that Gurgaon tehsil faced, restricting any possible improvement in agricultural production. Comparisons are often drawn with

Faridabad tehsil in this regard. Haryana became a state of India on 1 November 1966 and the new district of Faridabad, comprising the tehsils of Ballabhgarh and Palwal, was carved out of Gurgaon district on 15 August 1979.

The 1960s were the watershed years after independence. For our generation, born towards the end of it or later, this was the last decade of history that we got to know from literature. India gradually got used to the realities of freedom after the initial euphoria of independence, which came with the wounds of Partition. The decade saw distinctive regimes under three prime ministers, Jawaharlal Nehru, Lal Bahadur Shastri and Indira Gandhi. Interestingly, the prologue of Gurgaon's story can be traced back to that time, though the city we know of came into being in the 1990s. There was a conscious paradigm shift in the 1990s in economic policies from what was conceived in the 1960s. In that sense, the city touches both decades and two diverse paradigms.

The fragile polity in the 1990s, with different ideological positions of multiple governments, was somewhat reminiscent of the three different regimes in the 1960s, leading to methodological shifts in governance and party politics. Both were periods of transition. Worldviews changed even within the given political position. The Nehru-Shastri methods of the welfare state model were not similar to that of Indira Gandhi, and the three had diverse priorities and contexts. In fact, Shastri was quite different from Nehru in his approach, as was evident even in the mere one and a half years of his tenure.

Transition

Decisions taken then prepared the base for the development of Gurgaon. Of course, the 1990s ensued to mark the epoch. The Delhi Master Plan, the celebrated outcome of planning, was introduced in 1962 as a tangible follow-up to the Nehruvian vision. Its ambitious regional planning concept, that went on to form the basis of the National Capital Region Plan, was one of the contributing factors to Gurgaon's makeover.

Right from the days of the Constituent Assembly, Nehru had openly expressed an interest in comprehensive planning, a version of which was articulated in the Delhi Master Plan. The Plan began with a redistributive paradigm: the government acquired the land and redistributed it through a detailed land use plan, in consonance with the ideals of the welfare state at that time. The land use plan indicated the purpose or activity permissible in a plot of land. The Ford Foundation team led by Albert Mayer chalked out the Master Plan. A North American planner, Meyer held the idea that such a plan should be 'regional'. The Master Plan of Delhi, therefore, encompassed adjoining towns like Ghaziabad, Meerut, Sonipat, Rohtak, Faridabad and Gurgaon. The strategy was to develop these towns as counter-magnets to Delhi, spatially separated by 'green belts', so that urban expansion and unnecessary influx to the main city would be checked.

The expectations from the Master Plan were high even before it was ready. A retired senior official from the DDA (Delhi Development Authority) who used to teach with me, had been one of the young planners in the team. Once, he said, 'Panditji used to visit the office when we all were drawing up the Plan. He would drop in during evening hours and ask us to explain the proposal map.' Today, it seems unreal to hear about such keen interest, direct interaction and accessibility of the leaders of that era!

Nevertheless, the Delhi Master Plan championed the cause of 'planned' urbanization. Its introduction coincided with the Third Five Year Plan (1961–66) focussing on urbanization for the first time in post-independence India. The DDA acquired land through the Land Acquisition Act for 'public purpose'. It was perhaps the largest 'land nationalization' for urban development in independent India. The land was to be developed, leased and auctioned by the DDA and the surplus would be pumped into providing infrastructure. The DDA was supposed to build, develop and lease housing. The city would be built by the state.[1] Although a part of the regional dimension of the Delhi Master Plan in 1962, Gurgaon was identified as a weak spot as far as development potential was concerned. It would take at least two more decades to see significant development in Gurgaon.

The whole exercise of state-controlled urban development eventually pushed private developers like Delhi Land and Finance (DLF) out of Delhi. Recently, I was looking at the DLF website where certain milestones of the company were marked. DLF was established in 1946 and between 1950 and 1964, it developed 22 urban colonies in Delhi including Hauz Khas, South Extension, Model Town and Greater Kailash.

Transition

With the DDA's emergence as the sole 'developer' and housing provider, real estate companies like DLF gradually shifted out of Delhi. DLF initially moved its business to Faridabad, but with little luck. It was in Gurgaon that it finally found huge success. In the early 1990s, residents used to refer to the newer parts of Gurgaon as DLF. 'Where do you stay?' would be inevitably answered with 'DLF'. People related the place with the company to that extent! Perhaps it was more prestigious to say that one lived in DLF than in Gurgaon, because there was not much positivity associated with the then Gurgaon in any case.

∞

Lal Bahadur Shastri's famous slogan, *Jai Jawan, Jai Kisan*, also has relevance in this discussion. The Third Five-Year Plan (1961–66) underlined two important, and perhaps contradictory, visions: industrialization and the improvement of the condition of peasants across the country. The years 1965–66 steered India into the Green Revolution. Gurgaon, despite being in the midst of the agricultural upsurge in Punjab and, later, in Haryana, could not be a part of it. The subsequent irreversible shift away from agriculture in Gurgaon began during the later part of Indira Gandhi's term, especially with the establishment of the Maruti factory.

D.K. Rangnekar wrote an insightful piece in July 1964 in *Economic Weekly* (presently *Economic and Political Weekly*) on the transitional phases of the Nehru-Shastri era and the related dilemmas.[2] He was a known public intellectual and the editor of *The Economic Times* from the early 1960s to the 1980s, and later of *Business Standard* till his early demise. Rangnekar considered land reform and land ceiling to be major issues for necessary institutional modifications in the agrarian sector. Land reform, ceiling on landholding and agricultural cooperatives were part of the Congress' agenda for years, and Nehru's idea of joint cooperative farming was endorsed by the Congress party at its Nagpur session in 1958. Yet, elementary land reform legislations were not implemented in many parts of the country till the mid-1960s. Since a majority of people depended on agriculture, which also contributed a major chunk to the national income, a lot was left to be done. Therefore, focussing on agriculture and industry simultaneously could be a complicated matter for the Third Five-Year Plan.

Since then, the agriculture-industry paradox has surfaced on a number of occasions. The desperate push for industrialization in West Bengal towards the end of the three-decade-long Left Front rule led to an industry-agriculture conflict in 2007–08, against the backdrop of protests in Singur surrounding Tata's Nano factory. Land reform in Bengal, initiated by the Left Front government after 1977, had resulted in smaller landholdings redistributed to a large number of landowners. Besides the issue of fertile land, the presence of too many stakeholders increased the complexity of the matter in Singur.

Urbanization in Gurgaon did not have the problems of

Transition

Singur because of the not-so-fertile land and relatively large landholdings in the absence of land reform. The Land Ceiling Act, introduced in the early 1970s by the central government in place of complete land reform, also gave a backhanded incentive to Gurgaon's urbanization.

⁂

I was pleasantly surprised to find the historical gazetteer of Gurgaon district on the website of the Department of Revenue and Disaster Management of the government of Haryana. It is a worthy attempt to store such documents online for free access to interested people. Perhaps, historical maps along with gazetteers, too, can be archived in the concerned district's website.

The Gurgaon District Gazetteer (1910) indicates that at the beginning of the twentieth century, about 61 per cent of the population of the district was dependent on agriculture and over 90 per cent among them were owners or their dependents.[3] Following that, the district changed its configuration a number of times, and continued to be a place for 'peasant proprietors' till the 1980s.[4] After 70 years, the dependence on agriculture seemed to have increased. According to the District Gazetteer (1983), the economic sustenance of about 80 per cent of the people in Gurgaon depended on agriculture through direct cultivation, and through subsidiary or allied occupations. Gurgaon was considered to be a 'poor district' populated by a number of 'peasant proprietors owning small holdings', who would have tilled the land for others. In that case, many owners did not cultivate their own land. Hiring labour was not the usual practice here for general agricultural operations, except by certain communities like the Rajput, whose women were not used to support in the field.[5]

Till the time Gurgaon was an agriculture-based district, it was not considered to be an affluent place. On the contrary, Haryana has often been seen as a relatively 'rich' state of 'commercial farmers with medium-sized landholdings'. As per the Census 2011, even when urbanization in Haryana was higher than the country's average, around two-third of people in the state lived in rural settings.[6] However, Gurgaon's story has been different from the rest of the state in that sense.

From the beginning, Gurgaon did not really have favourable conditions for cultivation, compared to other major parts of Haryana known for rich agricultural produce. Less arable soil, coupled with inadequate rainfall, affected agricultural productivity in the district. Gurgaon also falls in an arid zone with low annual rainfall, which is within a range of 500–600 mm based on last three decades of rainfall data.[7] The considerable depth of groundwater level and poor water quality caused by salinity and alkalinity were also not suitable for agriculture.[8]

River Yamuna demarcated the eastern boundary of Haryana and that of the erstwhile Gurgaon district, before Faridabad district was carved out in the late 1970s. The Aravalli ridge to the eastern edge of the district demarcates

Faridabad and, for that matter, Delhi from present-day Gurgaon. The topography here is also quite different from the vast plains of Haryana, with no major river present in the district. In fact, the Aravalli divides two contrasting regions: the eastern alluvial plain, now in Faridabad and surroundings, and the western part of Gurgaon and beyond, comprising hilly terrain and sand dune areas. Only 28 per cent of the cultivable area was sown in the district at that time.[9]

During the Third Five-Year Plan (1961–66), to boost agriculture, irrigation was given a priority. To make Gurgaon sufficiently arable, irrigation was required, but the absence of any major river made that difficult. Gurgaon Canal was, thus, planned in the late 1960s to channelize Yamuna water from Faridabad.[10] The then Uttar Pradesh (UP) government objected to the original take-off point from Agra Canal, to be fed from the Yamuna River at Okhla, and the project was revised. The draft minutes of the meeting between the chief engineers and technical representatives of UP, Punjab and Rajasthan, that took place on 8 June 1955 at the office of the Chairman, Central Water and Power Commission, are available on the Web.[11] The shifting of the canal alignment down south, in turn, bypassed the present city of Gurgaon from its direct command area. On the contrary, Faridabad and its adjoining region to the east were provided with direct irrigation facilities right from the beginning.

This came to be reflected in the divergent nature of development in Gurgaon and Faridabad over the years. Bibek Debroy and Laveesh Bhandari from Delhi have captured this phenomenon in a well-researched working paper prepared for the Law and Economy in India Project at Stanford University.[12] Until June 2019, Debroy, an eminent economist, was one of the members of NITI Aayog, the new avatar of the former Planning Commission. Their paper identified many such reasons for the initial spurt in urbanization towards Faridabad. One of the interesting observations, among others, to come out of their work was the lack of agricultural productivity and large landholdings in Gurgaon. The average landholding in Gurgaon was 6.1 acres in 1980–81, about 1.3 times that of Faridabad. As per the Agricultural Census 2000–01, the average landholding in Gurgaon came down to about 4.2 acres, similar to that of Faridabad in 1980–81, yet almost 70 per cent of the land area was almost 5 acres in size. This fact, I found later, has been reconfirmed in the biography of K.P. Singh, the head of DLF, in his discussions on land acquisition around the same time.

Let me summarize the story so far. Till the 1970s, Gurgaon was a place with a rural agrarian base, but with low agricultural productivity on account of the not-very-fertile land. Additionally, the area was not supported with irrigation systems as well. The business-as-usual condition was far from satisfactory, leaving scope for more profitable utilization of land for other purposes. At that time, three Acts were introduced within a short period of time, breathing fresh air into the simmering possibilities of transition.

Transition

The Haryana Ceiling on landholdings Act 1972, Haryana Development and Regulations of Urban Areas Act (HDRUA) 1975 (30 January), the Urban Land (Ceiling and Regulation) Act [ULCRA] 1976 (17 February) and the Haryana Urban Development Authority (HUDA) Act 1977 were introduced within a short period of time. All these acts, rules and guidelines left certain gaps and loopholes and in effect, created a condition of exception, which Gurgaon development took full advantage of. Shubhra Gurunani, a faculty member in the Department of Anthropology at York University, has captured how Gurgaon became 'a zone of exemption' and consequential urbanization happened out of 'flexible planning'.[13] The development was the result of the varied outcomes of fluid negotiations and the underlying purpose, to accumulate capital. Both were totally different from the way planning was seen as a rationalist instrumentation in Delhi.

Besides the introduction of these three Acts, the Punjab Pre-emption Act of 1913 was repealed around this time. The Act empowered any family member to stake a claim on a property, years after it had been duly sold by the legal owner. Such a clause posed an imminent threat to real estate developers who had been toying with the idea of large projects in Gurgaon. In his autobiographical book, K.P. Singh talked about how he negotiated with powerful decision-makers to repeal this Act.

> I met bureaucrats and politicians to explain the logic of why Haryana could not afford to continue to have

this law [Punjab Pre-emption Act of 1913] on its statute books. Even though everyone I spoke to accepted my contention in principle, they were hesitant to do anything about changing the law because no one wanted to be seen doing anything that would help private developers in politically sensitive Haryana. But I kept on trying to convince them that such a law would seriously retard the development of the state. It took time but after scores of meetings, things finally started moving and in due course the Punjab Pre-emption Act of 1913 was repealed.[14]

The legislation regarding the 'controlled area' was introduced in the Punjab Scheduled Roads and Controlled Areas Restriction of Unregulated Development Act 1963. Under this Act, the Government could notify a 'controlled area' that was 'adjacent to and within a distance of a) eight kilometres on the outer sides of the boundary of any town, or, b) two kilometres on the outer sides of the boundary of any industrial or housing estate, public institution or an ancient and historical monument'.[15] Ninety-four roads were listed in the schedule. The Town and Country Planning Organization (TCPO) was entrusted with the preparation of the plans indicating the 'controlled area' with proposed 'restrictions and conditions'. The plans were then to be submitted to the government.

This Act, greatly in use in the 1970s, was significant in the early phases of Gurgaon's development initiated by HUDA.

With an objective 'to prevent haphazard and substandard development along scheduled roads and in controlled areas', it created a development pattern in which roads were used as armatures. First, a road was laid to connect two points; in most of the cases those would be two existing roads. Then, assorted enclaves would come up, plugging into such an armature. This has been the ongoing urbanization process in Gurgaon.

The Department of Town and Country Planning, government of Haryana website, I am pleasantly surprised, is very informative in this regard.[16] Interestingly, Gurgaon has the highest number of notifications of controlled areas, compared to other cities in Haryana. One hundred and thirteen notifications can be found in Gurgaon, out of 502 notifications all over the state, at the time of writing this book. This certainly indicates that the incremental urbanization of Gurgaon has been pushing the boundary of the controlled areas. At the outset, up to 8 km outside the Gurgaon municipal town limit was identified as a controlled area. Land use pattern was specified for this area, including about 50 villages and their adjoining agricultural land.[17] Once the private developers started acquiring land, many techniques came into play for land amalgamation and consolidation.

At that time, DLF and the Ansals were the primary players and the real estate mega-production started with DLF Phase-I and Palam Vihar. Multiple techniques, from local-level political negotiations to financial compensation and coercion by private developers, were adopted for land consolidation, rather successfully. Ahirs, traditional milkmen, were the major community here, but they were not so close-knit. The other prominent group was the Jat community and it is a known fact now that K.P. Singh of DLF, a Jat himself, could negotiate with the community very well, in order to maximize the land acquisition. Unlike Singur in Bengal, where the then state government was very eager to help the Tatas acquire land, resulting in a political uproar, here the government made strategic facilitation of the process in a comparatively quiet manner.

While purchasing land within the controlled area, developers often bought agricultural parcels outside it as well and created an enclave under their brand. This happened because land outside the controlled area was cheaper. The consolidation of large enclaves or land parcels also happened by combining a portion of land within the controlled area and the rest outside it. In turn, the developer was able to sell the property at a much higher price. For buyers, too, it was a win-win situation, as the average price of each plot or flat would come down. The biggest casualty of the process was the effort of regulating urbanization within a boundary. After one and a half decades of this land-banking process, by the mid-1990s, the entire district of Gurgaon became a controlled area. The main thrust of real estate started after that.

One of my students worked on a planning thesis on the urban fringe development of Indore. A similar process was happening there as well. Perhaps, this is now a systemic subversion of what is conceptualized as classical land use zoning, surviving on a redistributive state-driven model. It is time to relook at such methods and tools of planning.

A further twist in the tale was the concept of the 'power of relaxation' in the 1963 Act. A couple of provisions were added to it to for manipulation and advantage.[18] The government was empowered to relax already notified land use to uphold 'public interest'. Such changes could be made with the permission of the director, Town and Country Planning, on payment of certain 'conversion charges'.

With such options, planning in Gurgaon became an operation of tactical negotiation and collusion. The first step was to declare the land unproductive, followed by altering the land use through the 'power of relaxation', and finally, to acquire it by paying hefty compensation. It helped the developer, the decision-maker and often the seller in more ways than one. Instead of a controlled area to contain urbanization, it was the other way round: urbanization was adjusting the limit of control.

The Haryana Ceiling on Land Holdings Act 1972 was the precursor to the ULCRA 1976. The 1972 Act coined a term called 'permissible area', an area that the property owner was allowed to hold. A family of five was considered to be the primary unit. For such a family, landholding was not to exceed 53.9 acres (21.8 hectares) and to be determined by the type of irrigation, yields of crop and other factors. For example, a family could hold about 18 acres (7.25 hectares) of two-crop land under 'assured' irrigation and almost 27 acres (10.9 hectares) of the single-crop-land.

Irrigation by perennial or seasonal canals, by private tube-well or pumping, also assured the agricultural yield and therefore, decided the classification of land. In turn, the upper limit of holdings was to be calculated on the classification. For each additional member of a family, the permissible area could also be increased by one-fifth of that of the primary unit of a family, provided that such a landholding shall not exceed twice the permissible area of the primary unit of a family.

As per this Act, unreliable irrigation and infertile land in Gurgaon might have contributed to larger holdings of agricultural land. Eventually, the joint family structure was also affected and dissolved because of the land-per-family concept of the Act. Surplus land would be acquired by the state government for 'public purpose'. Interestingly, certain types of land owned by, or vested in the state government or the central government, were not included in the Act. Around 1980–81, as mentioned earlier, about 70 per cent of land in Gurgaon was about 5–7.5 acres (2–3 hectares) after the implementation of the Act. Such large land parcels also increased the ease of development because the developer had to deal with fewer landowners.

To put this land size in perspective, the land of Saket District Centre in South Delhi is a little over 54 acres, almost similar to the maximum permissible landholding of one typical family. South City complex, an upmarket mixed-use development in Kolkata is about 31.1 acres, little over half of the same landholding. The plot area of ITC Laburnum, an iconic housing enclave in Gurgaon, is about 12.5 acres, one-fourth of this landholding. If Gurgaon is about the conversion of agricultural parcel into floor area, it is important to relate the scale and size of land and how much development that land can accommodate.

The Haryana Development and Regulations of Urban Areas Act (HDRUA) 1975 and the HUDA Act 1977 followed soon. HDRUA 1975 was particularly unique to the state and, in many ways, was instrumental in shaping Gurgaon. In Haryana, competent authorities can permit participation of private developers, colonizers and builders to assemble parcels of land beyond the land ceiling limit.[19] The Act, introduced on 30 January 1975, was supposed 'to regulate the use of land in order to prevent ill-planned and haphazard urbanization in or around towns in the State of Haryana'. It outlined the procedures for acquiring a 'licence' for the developers or colonizers along with the possible conditions for exemptions.[20]

Simultaneously, a window was opened for obtaining a licence for those who had not taken permission earlier, under the 1963 Act. In other words, certain irregularities were ratified and manipulations initiated in earlier Acts were further strengthened—pay and develop! Interestingly, on paper, all the while, the chief of the state-level planning organization was the one who endorsed all such issues.

In November 1980, the chief secretary of the government

of Haryana wrote to all concerned officials regarding the selection of sites and acquisition of land by government departments and corporate bodies and others. The letter said:

> [B]efore making selection of any site, or starting land acquisition proceedings or issuing No Objection Certificates for land acquisition involving change of land use in the Controlled Areas, prior consultation with the department of Town & Country Planning must be held.[21]

However, where the Development Plans had not been published, a decision on the application for change in land use was to be taken at the level of the government. The permission for development came with certain compliances regarding development and maintenance, reservations and limit of profit, among others.[22] The external development charges leading to the plot were to be paid to HUDA on a gross area basis—the larger the development, the higher the charges. Also, a separate account was to be opened for depositing 30 per cent of the proceeds of the land sale, which would be used for development and maintenance of the completed colony for five years. A certain number of plots and flats were to be reserved for Economically Weaker Section (EWS) categories, including domestic helpers.

The number and size of houses and plots, however, varied over time. Twenty-five per cent of the total plots in plotted residential areas were to be allotted under the 'No Profits No Loss' category and to be sold at the rate prescribed by the director. These plots seemed to be for the use of influential people in the machinery. A 'limit' of 15 per cent profit on the total project cost was fixed, with excess profit to be returned to the state. Some of these rules, one may feel, were ascertained to address certain social and economic needs. Yet, there were enough loopholes and interpretations for further twists and turns.

At that juncture, the ULCRA was enacted by the Government of India simultaneously in 11 states in February 1976. By the end of the 1980s, the Act covered over 73 urban agglomerations. Haryana was one such state and the Act, in a different way, helped urban development in Gurgaon take off. The basic objectives of this Act seemed reasonable: to introduce a certain order in urbanization, to check the speculation of land and restrict its price and to promote the construction of low income housing.[23] To achieve these objectives, the law framed a threefold measure: a ceiling on the vacant landholdings of individuals or companies, a limitation on the size of the dwelling units to be built on the plot in future, and regulation of the transfer of urban property.

Besides cities, this Act also encompassed urban agglomerations, generally identified by a 5-km belt around the city, where urbanization had often been seen engulfing prime agricultural land. In fact, such an inverse relationship between peri-urban development and agricultural land around the urban area continues till date, despite many attempts by urban planners to 'control' it.

The NCR, with Delhi and the surrounding six ring towns, were brought under ULCRA. As a planning strategy, a buffer zone was to be maintained as the separator between the ring towns and the main city of Delhi, to curb urban sprawl. Spread across three different states, it was difficult to administer the NCR agglomeration. The very nature of the jurisdictional ambiguity of the NCR made ULCRA an advantage and not the limiting factor for urbanization. The adjoining land, where ULCRA would be applied, was kept vacant in the Development Plan of Gurgaon.

Over and above, the Act also exempted certain land uses like industrial, educational, institutional and health facilities. Because of the Municipal Council status of Gurgaon, land matters were decided by the chief minister directly. The situation was fluid for a lot of negotiations. Thus, these swatches of land were imminently open to interpretations and manipulations. Large areas of land changed hands in Gurgaon in those areas. DLF obtained a licence in 1981 to make housing colonies and acquired about 3,500 acres of land.

Actual operations, one can anticipate, were not so straightforward. Any successful operator in Gurgaon, be it a patwari, technocrat or developer, had to master the art of favourably manipulating these Acts under the aegis of the final decision-makers. Gurgaon also has an exceptional set of operators known as 'CLU consultant', where CLU stands for Change in Land Use.

Of late, while browsing through the TCPO website, I

realized that three Development Plans (for 2012, 2015 and 2013) had been finalized within a period of less than six years, from February 2007 to November 2012. Not only that, the 2013 Plan had been further amended in the beginning of 2017. Recent amendments, by and large, had been made to accommodate transit-oriented development possibilities within and around DLF sectors, which were opened up by the Rapid Metro system under DLF. One key modification was made to allow 'tradable FAR' for 24-m- and 18-m-wide roads, green belts and open space zones. In other words, incentives were handed out for physical infrastructure like roads and socio-environmental facilities like green belts, which now could be counted for FAR calculations. How could such a need have arisen now? We shall have to wait to see implications of these in future.

The later part of 2011 saw the removal of the ceiling on land ownership by a person or entity in the case of non-agricultural land in urban and industrial zones. As the then media reports suggested, this move would have brought 'relief' to private developers. Otherwise, the surreptitious practice of floating different entities to assemble land parcels for housing enclaves or townships was quite common in the state.

I taught for a little over a decade in an architecture college located near present-day sectors 55 and 56. Like many others, I have seen that part of Gurgaon evolve. In early 2000, a deserted wide Golf Course Road was the main connection with Mehrauli-Gurgaon Road (MG Road), the prime route to South Delhi. At that time, an incomplete Golf Course Road was under construction and would vanish after Sector 56, on the approach from the Golf Club side. Traces of agriculture and farming communities could be seen; the grazing land for animals was fast diminishing. Vehicles were few and far between; it was a road to test the speed of cars. I was among those who used to leave the college last, most of the time accompanied by a group of students who lived in Gurgaon temporarily. The majority of them were from outside Gurgaon and used to stay together in groups in nearby rented accommodations.

'Sir, please don't drive so fast. By the time our motorbikes reach the main street, your car is already out of sight,' Baikunth, a student of mine, cautioned me. 'There are many animals on the road, they suddenly run out in front of cars and create problems.' I was touched by their concern and remember their words even after 15–16 years. What used be a field has become a wide road. At that time, one could see more animals on the road than cars!

For the development of sectors 55 and 56, the lands of Ved Pal, Ramprakash and many other farmers from Wazirabad and Haiderpur villages were taken away by HUDA. However, no plots were offered to them in compensation as promised. Finally, some of them moved court and towards the end of 2011, the High Court of Punjab and Haryana gave its verdict in favour of the farmers.[24] The majority of such displaced persons, the two-judge Bench observed, were usually 'small farmers', rarely consulted before the land acquisition process and in turn, were 'always inadequately compensated'. In this way, most of these ousted farmers became 'considerably poorer than before', the Hon'ble judges opined. These interpretations underlined the inadequacy of the rehabilitation and resettlement policy. Also, HUDA, despite being asked by the Court, could not produce the data and the documents on the number of plots carved out from sectors 55 and 56, and how many of those were made available for the displaced community. Excerpts of the court verdict made very pertinent points:[25]

> The basic purpose of quickly settling the oustees appears to be a complete failure. The escalating crisis of displacement have [sic] been aggravated by the displacement of wholesale communities and houses of village is [sic] invariable part of implementation of the urban projects.
>
> The respondents [HUDA] are directed to specifically float allotment scheme before putting it to the general public for allotment of plots and the size as may be available depending upon the oustee policies. If the plots are not available in the sector for which the land has been acquired, special efforts be made to settle the oustees in other nearby sectors and also specifically enforce the oustee policies to avoid unnecessary future litigation.

Many farmers and original landowners often favoured private developers more than HUDA. Financial negotiations and political and power coercions, put together, created a formidable situation for individual farmers. Most of them were not united enough to resist. A different situation prevails these days, when the government is liable to pay more than the market price for land under the Right to Fair Compensation and Transparency in Land Acquisition, Rehabilitation and Resettlement Act 2013 of Haryana. Now, farmers are, by and large, ready to sell their land for a higher price, but developers are not showing interest in buying acquired land from government agencies like HUDA.

A headline in *Hindustan Times* in September 2016 said: 'High cost of land acquisition slows down new Huda projects in Gurgaon.'[26] The report suggested that the compensation paid to farmers for the ongoing land acquisition in sectors 68 to 80, was almost ₹10 crore per acre, whereas the market rate was around ₹5 crore per acre. The land was being acquired to build a road connecting Southern Peripheral Road (SPR) and Delhi-Jaipur National Highway 48. But why was HUDA trying to acquire land to build roads while reportedly facing a cash crunch?

As mentioned earlier, the process of development here often begins with making important roads, then the assorted enclaves come up along the road. This plug and play method of development has been the legitimate source of income for HUDA as well. For obvious reasons but in covert ways, it would also interest certain important people in the decision-making process. With the slowdown in the real estate sector, private developers were seemingly not so keen on buying land in Gurgaon even at the market price, the crisis was thus created. However, in contrast to the last story of the court case for the land between the farmers and HUDA, farmers were at least willing to sell their land to HUDA due to higher compensation for land acquisition.

HUDA acquires land which is then bought by private developers, thus ensuring an income for them. Problems arise in the case of large green spaces, playgrounds, water bodies, forest belts, etc. Such spaces do not have an immediate monetary value attached. Therefore, to acquire land to provide social and environmental facilities would always pinch any money-making organization and private developers. Thus, it would be especially difficult for HUDA to acquire such land while facing a money crunch. The Authority had to let go of the acquisition of around 1,290 acres of land allocated for large public parks and a stadium among other open spaces under the Gurgaon-Manesar Urban Complex Master Plan 2031. 'We had to drop the plan as it would cost more than ₹6,000 crore to acquire this land under the new rules. However, this area will remain an open space because the zoning has not been changed,' the Land Acquisition Officer (LAO) of HUDA reportedly said.[27]

However, such moves shall have telling impacts on the quality of life of residents. In addition to that, if the government authority does not provide open spaces, how shall we expect the private developers to do so? HUDA has been toying with alternative ideas of collaboration with farmers through land-pooling or TDR (Transfer of Development Rights) to address this issue. Especially after the land-pooling for the Amravati capital complex in Telangana was publicized, such possibilities have come to the fore.

~

Gurgaon has been a joint development model between the private and the public. To begin with, the department of Town and Country Planning of Haryana prepared a Development Plan for the large Gurgaon Township that envisaged new urban areas on 11,243 acres (4,550 hectares), of which a little over 64 per cent would be residential and the rest was to be utilized for industrial, commercial and public/semi-public use etc.[28] More than half of the new residential area was to be set up by HUDA, with land acquired from farmers at very low prices under the Land Acquisition Act 1894. The rest would be developed by private real estate companies. HUDA established the residential areas with plots ranging from 50 to 600 sq. m in size and the prices were low by market standards.

The initial land banking process by private developers was different. During 1980–81, K.P. Singh of DLF and Sushil Ansal of Ansal Group, another leading Delhi-based real estate developer, got the licence to acquire land to build DLF colonies and Palam Vihar respectively. Sushil Ansal was quoted elsewhere, saying that Singh had the ability to convince officials. Singh also mentioned in his autobiography that the two of them, accompanied by Ramesh Chandra, used to visit Chandigarh to lobby with officials and politicians. Chandra was the chairman of Unitech, the third most important real estate player in Gurgaon at that time. Unitech's quality delivery of certain landmark projects in Gurgaon, and often-talked-about professional management structure, many believed, contributed to the group's meteoric rise until a few years back, when the company faced legal action and a sharp downfall thereafter.

DLF acquired land directly from farmers in the 1980s. In fact, its first piece of land was acquired in October 1980 to set off the process. K.P. Singh describes the process and the tactics in great detail in his autobiographical account. The following anecdote sums it up very well.

> When you make an effort to hold hands with your partners, they always back you. Mohar Singh, for instance, had around ten acres of barren land in Gurgaon. He was happy to get `5 million for it. All his life, he had not even seen `10,000 in cash. I told him that he would gain if he deposited the entire amount back with DLF to make it grow. He readily agreed. Touched by his trusting attitude, I asked him if we could help in some way. Mohar Singh said he would be glad if DLF employed his son as a watchman. Here was the ultimate irony: someone who had five million rupees was asking me to get his son a menial job. I desperately wanted that money to develop land and all

it required was one small favour from me. I got his son employed by DLF. A job, however ordinary, made them feel useful and secure. We were dealing with villagers with such modest dreams.[29]

The key tactics were twofold: to build interpersonal relations with the farmers to attain a certain comfort level for negotiations, and to ensure that the land transaction was beneficial to all parties—seller, buyer and the end-user. K.P. Singh, a Jat hailing from a farming family of Bulandshahr, had served in the army in his early days before getting involved in the real estate business. Singh's caste as well as his rural and army background helped him get close to the peasant families of Gurgaon. It was important to establish such a rapport with the community of farmers who held land as a part and parcel of their way of life and never had the practice of selling it.

In such a socio-occupational condition, DLF acquired about 3,500 acres of land. If Singh is to be believed, the initial price paid for the land was around ₹5 lakh per acre (₹125 per sq. m). Considering each family had about 4–5 acres, over 700 families were to be negotiated with. The land in Gurgaon, as I have mentioned earlier, was not very productive and faced severe water shortage. DLF promised to provide farmers ten times more land elsewhere, with better agricultural yield and security in lieu of their not-so-fertile land parcels in Gurgaon. Each family profile was recorded by DLF with the quantity and quality of land they owned, their personal traits and the problems they faced. Singh was able to establish proximity with the peasant families by attending birthday parties, settling family disputes, helping with the school admission of children and medical assistance, among other things.

This rigorous networking undertaken by Singh and DLF, was not merely restricted to the farmers. The overarching reach had the patwari on one end and the chief minister on the other. DLF bought land, parcel by parcel, handed over the money and then convinced the farmers to invest in DLF for financial benefits. Seeing the success achieved by the company in Gurgaon, some humorously nicknamed DLF 'Damn Lucky Fellow'. However, it might not be always a smooth affair. All said and done, it was a roaring success story of private land acquisition.

Indian polity at that juncture was witnessing a key moment in post-independence history. The Emergency lasted for 21 months (25 June 1975 to 21 March 1977). Once the Emergency was lifted and a fresh mandate was sought, for the first time, a non-Congress government in the form of Janata Party wrested the power at the Centre. Janata Party formed an alliance with the opposition parties, which lasted a little less than three years (March 1977 to January 1980), before Congress, under the leadership of Indira Gandhi, came back to form the Union government.

An important name of that time was Bansi Lal (1927–2006), the four-time chief minister of Haryana. He was also one of the key players in the overall development of

Haryana. The state of Haryana was created in 1966. He became its chief minister in 1968 and continued for the next term till he was brought to the central ministry in 1975. He was again at the helm of affairs in the state for two shorter periods, 1985–87 and 1996–99. Before his last term as chief minister, Bansi Lal parted ways with the Congress and formed the Haryana Vikas Party in 1996, which finally merged with the Congress in October 2004. Many believe that Bansi Lal was the architect of Haryana that we see today. The growth story of Gurgaon, too, began in his time.

I still remember seeing a small photograph of Bansi Lal in *Jugantar*, a popular Bengali daily during our childhood, which was closed down many years ago. *Jugantar*, under the *Amrita Bazaar Patrika* group, and *Ananda Bazar Patrika* were the two most popular vernacular newspapers of that time. *Jugantar* had carried a small news report on Bansi Lal's induction as the defence minister at the Centre, from December 1975 to March 1977. Even before becoming a Union minister, he was known for his proximity to Sanjay Gandhi, the younger maverick son of the then prime minister Indira Gandhi. Bansi Lal's assistance to Sanjay Gandhi in setting up Maruti is well known and documented. I looked up some of the literature of that time to understand the Maruti episode and referred to two veteran journalists' works extensively: Kuldip Nayar's book on the Emergency and Vinod Mehta's book on Sanjay Gandhi. Besides those, Maruti Suzuki's chairman, R.C. Bhargava's book was also a good source for someone interested in knowing about this incredible growth story.[30]

Transition

Sanjay Gandhi was a passionate automobile lover. He had apprenticed with the car manufacturer Rolls Royce Motors for three years and had brought back to India a noble, yet seemingly impossible, idea—of making a 'people's car'. Towards the end of 1970, the Central government issued a letter of intent to Maruti Ltd to produce 50,000 cars annually. At that time, Sanjay was the managing director of Maruti. With the letter, his next target was to arrange for land and finance. Bansi Lal offered land for the factory, which had to be located close to Lutyens' Delhi where Sanjay Gandhi stayed in the prime minister's house. The proximity would then enable him to visit the factory easily. Accordingly, more than 400 acres of land were identified on the highway. It appears from the descriptions of both the journalists that the offered land parcel had sufficient agricultural activities on it and adequate compensation was not given to the farmers in return. Besides that, the land was located right next to a military ammunition depot.

On one hand, the proposed factory would pose a security threat, and on the other, it would flout the existing rule that prohibited any construction within 1,000 m of an ammunition depot. Finally, the depot was shifted and the factory was established, following the incorporation of Maruti Motors Limited in the middle of 1971. In November 1972, a prototype car was unveiled and 'the people's car' was supposed to hit the road by the middle of the next year with an expected price tag of ₹11,300.[31] At that time, three companies in the Indian automobile industry manufactured iconic car models of their own: Hindustan Motors' Ambassador, Premier Automobiles' Premier Padmini and Standard Motors' Standard Herald. The idea of Maruti came with a dash of hope for middle-class Indians, who could now aspire to possess a car.

The end of Emergency ushered in the new Janata Party coalition and, with that, a series of enquiries related to Maruti. In March 1978, the High Court of Punjab and Haryana ordered the winding up of Maruti Motors. By that time, not more than 40 Maruti cars might have been manufactured. In hindsight, we know that had the Maruti venture ended with that order, it would have been a disaster.

The Maruti story reminds me of the Tata initiative, of manufacturing another 'people's car' three decades later. The Tata Nano factory was established in West Bengal, but the project met with severe land agitation, leading to massive political turmoil in West Bengal. The end of 34 years of Left rule in Bengal was triggered by the 'Nano Agitation'. In August 2016, the Honourable Supreme Court, quashed the acquisition of land in Singur for the Tata Motors project and directed that the acquired land be returned to the farmers. Tata finally shifted its factory to Gujarat and produced the Nano out of its factory there, but the setback that the project had received right at the beginning could not be truly overcome.

Fortunately, Maruti was revived with the incorporation of Maruti Udyog Limited in February 1981 as a 100 per cent government-owned company. The project eventually went

Transition

on to revolutionize the Indian automobile industry.

By that time, the Janata Party government had been overturned through a fresh election, the Indira Gandhi-led Congress government had wrested back power and Sanjay Gandhi had lost his life in an air crash in June 1980. Soon after, the possibilities of reviving Maruti were explored. It was observed that the project's rejuvenation would require a joint venture with a foreign technology provider and the minimum production volume of one lakh cars in a year.[32] Indira Gandhi brought in some visionaries to manage the Maruti Udyog Limited, which had been formed in 1981. The Japanese car giant Suzuki Motor Corporation was roped in as the foreign joint venture partner in 1982.

Despite the then closed market of India, Maruti received the right to import fully built-up Suzuki cars in the first two years. The initial target was to use one-third indigenous parts, which was upsetting for the other local car manufacturers. Finally, in 1983, the iconic Maruti 800 was released as India's first affordable car. By the end of 1983, local production commenced. The plant capacity in Gurgaon was augmented to 40,000 units in the next one year and was further amplified to one lakh units per annum by 1988. In 1992, once Suzuki Motor Corporation was allowed to increase its equity from 40 per cent to 50 per cent, Maruti ceased to be a public sector undertaking. Today, Maruti Suzuki is the biggest car player in the country.

In mid-1980s, I saw for the first time my neighbour driving the red-coloured, toy-like car in a suburb of West Bengal.

It was an amazing sight, witnessing something new on the road. I never thought at that time that the establishment of Maruti would mark the beginning of the urbanization process of Gurgaon, a place where I would work for over a decade. In fact, I did not know of Gurgaon at that time.

The next phase of Gurgaon's development went to the industrial sector, along with related residential and supporting infrastructure. Since 1981, urban Gurgaon has grown by leaps and bounds: according to Census, in 1981–91, the population growth was 36.3 per cent; in 1991–2001, it was 65.7 per cent; and in 2001–11, it reached 340.3 per cent. In other words, in the first decade of the millennium, Gurgaon's population more than tripled and the city witnessed the maximum growth. One reason could be that during this period, more area was included within the urban limit. Suddenly, Gurgaon changed in front of our eyes and we could not fathom what had happened!

Although the city was constructed in front of everyone there, no one realized how fast it had expanded. Many may still remember seeing the mustard fields in Phase III of the DLF areas located right after the Delhi border. At that time, the sector road within that locality was not contiguous — on one side, the road came from the National Highway and the other from MG Road. Since a large chunk of agricultural land was yet to be acquired, these two stretches ended abruptly without leading anywhere. For a long time, DLF Phase III existed in two parts, unconnected and disjointed even when the Gurgaon development project was at its peak!

Haryana's neo-liberal model of land acquisition, made directly by private companies with minimum state intervention, helped the process of urbanization. However, there were certain grey areas in that process as well. Local officers colluded with builders and artificially lowered the land value. State agencies gave notices for land acquisition and determined the compensation rates for the farmland. Then, private builders entered the scene and offered a higher price to the farmers than the rates given by the government. The farmers usually accepted the price of the private companies as it was more profitable than the acquisition rates meted out to them. Once a substantial chunk of land had been acquired by the private developers, official notices were withdrawn. That was the convoluted nexus between the public and private enterprises, aimed to hasten land grabbing. A number of Gurgaon residents mentioned such stories, which had also been reported elsewhere. In that sense, local discontentment among Gurgaon farmers was not very high, compared to many other places in the country. Sporadic protests, whenever those took place, were usually spearheaded by rich peasants without much involvement of landless farmers and, therefore, did not get critical mass and necessary momentum.

Private developers were required to pay heavy external development charges to HUDA and, apparently, little development was visible in the beginning. By 1986, HUDA had invested about 70 per cent of its external development funds on roads alone and had done very little for water, drains and sewerage. Developers were reluctant to pay the charges and by mid-1986, the state government served over 200 show-cause notices to most of the private developers, threatening to cancel licences. A report indicated that the developers filed court cases against the notice, leading to the suspension of development work in Gurgaon for two years. Finally, compromises were arrived at, licences were restored and land development began in 1988 'in a much better climate'.[33]

Gurgaon's transition, from a quiet agriculture-based rustic settlement to what we see today, began with Maruti and was subsequently triggered in the next phase by Genpact shifting their base there. Pramod Bhasin, former head of Genpact, says that when their office was moved to Gurgaon from Rafi Marg in Lutyens' Delhi, his employees asked him whether he had 'gone mad'. 'There were no roads, there were no shops, there were no restaurants and there was no traffic. In that sense, it was heaven,' Bhasin said, while speaking at a public gathering in India Habitat Centre in Delhi.

This transition was essentially the transformation of land and its use, but without any set land use planning. The change in ownership, consolidation of land and its changed urban use were spatial politics of land, which included the allocation of land amongst different, often competing uses, and the distributional outcomes of such decisions. Some would argue that allocative decisions form the very core of conventional urban planning, which in any case, had been missing in Gurgaon's story right from the beginning. The remarkable growth story of Gurgaon was ad hoc, assorted and full of turns and twists that eventually turned around the negatives in favour of development.

AMBITION

To Be Rich and Successful

> If we consider for a minute that a city has a life of a hundred years, Gurgaon is a small kid and has grown on its own without being put into a regular school. However, it showed to the nation a newer face of a city—one which had opted for denims when the rest of the country was wearing a dhoti.

Vishal put it in a rather interesting way while sipping his Italian soup with a complicated name. I preferred a cup of tea instead, my favourite, and trusted drink. We were at a restaurant in Galleria near his house in DLF Phase IV, discussing Gurgaon.

Vishal Aggarwal is a practising architect who has lived in Gurgaon for a long time. We have known each other for almost 20 years and taught together in an architecture college in the city for about a decade. His journey to Gurgaon began in the mid-1990s, when projects in construction and real estate sectors in Delhi were drying up. There was a sense of saturation in these sectors, leaving aside some opportunities that were not enough for newer generations to flourish.

At that point of time, the dot com business had already started, with Noida as its initial base. Somewhere around 1998, Gurgaon began emerging as a place with corporates like British Airways moving in, and Vishal felt that professionals like architects could get substantial work there. 'Luckily, I got work at that time because I had done some dot-com office interior projects,' he said.

Galleria, the location for our rendezvous, is an interesting combination of a low-height market and a tall office building showing off the ugly sight of the whole matrix of outdoor air-conditioning units. The two-storeyed market has a symmetrical layout with a central, open-to-sky court and a small circular water body and fountain, with four wide pathways leading to it. These paths are also lined with shops on both sides. A row of shops open to the outside areas facing the road and others open to the court at the centre. A report a couple of years back suggested that DLF Galleria has one of the costliest property rentals in the country, following Connaught Place and Khan Market, both of which are right in the middle of Lutyens' Delhi.[34]

With a neighbourhood feel to its spatial scale and well-maintained public spaces, the market showcases international brands and has pharmacies, electronics stores, beauty parlours and spas, grocery shops, gifts and book stores, and pet stores among others. A high footfall helps to attract international brands. It is also a preferred meet-up place with a variety of restaurants. The spacious arrangement with large open areas and the leisurely nature of its organization make it a successful public place different from many other malls in the city, which are housed within closed vertical structures.

'I happened to get in touch with GE, one of the forerunners in corporatizing Gurgaon and was appointed the architect for their main facilities. That was the magnet that drew me towards Gurgaon for work,' Vishal's voice brought me back to the conversation.

In the mid- to late 1990s, many young professionals like him in their late 20s and early 30s were drawn to Gurgaon to live and work. They, perhaps, could smell the aroma of cosmopolitan urbanity. Delhi was unaffordable to have a home of one's own and Gurgaon offered that opportunity, although at that time the place was underdeveloped. Many young people who worked in Gurgaon, decided to settle there. A 'glamour factor', of possessing a plotted house at a young age, was also a reason why Gurgaon became a choice by default. The property price in the city seemed very high, but in comparison to Delhi, it was affordable for those young professionals.

The 'ambition' of being able to afford a property, especially a plotted house, and securing a well-paid corporate job at a time when the economy was opening up, were two key factors that contributed to the influx of young people with software, core engineering, IT, management and similar specializations, to Gurgaon.

Similar reasons brought Latika Thukral, a former banker,

Ambition

to the city in 1996. After her marriage, she and her husband, both working in Delhi, stayed in a rented accommodation in Vasant Kunj for a while. When they were in search of a property of their own, very few options were available for them in Delhi. They finally opted for Gurgaon primarily because of its affordability. Though they paid a fairly high price for the property, compared to Delhi, it was 'viable' for them. In that sense, Gurgaon became a choice by default for a large section of its present population who typifies the most visible social milieu of the place.

These are the generic sub-plots within the story of Gurgaon and its people. Affordability and availability with respect to Delhi have been the most important thread that tied the initial migrants to the city. None of them really expected much at that point and, in turn, witnessed how things unfolded on the urban geography of Gurgaon. Spatial openness, low population density in the initial years and social groups of similar age and professional background were what made them interested in the place. Most of them were first-generation property owners, at a time when very few offices existed in the city. Whoever shifted there, wanted to buy a house instead of renting it. Thus, Gurgaon got its new citizens, a group of ambitious and aspirational youth who would be in their 50s by now.

Later, many offices shifted to Gurgaon and the city changed so fast that it transformed drastically before anyone could realize what was happening. GE capital was one organization that played a key role in this transformation.

The architectural work of GE Capital prompted people like Vishal to shift their base from West Delhi to Gurgaon, whereas having shifted to Gurgaon, Latika's husband also started to work for GE. The story of Maruti and DLF marked two crucial phases of 'transition' of the city and GE marked the beginning of the dot-com wave. Gurgaon became a place to pursue 'ambition'.

―

The way K.P. Singh convinced Jack Welch, CEO of GE, to locate their outsourcing office, GE Capital, in Gurgaon, is a well-known story. GE Capital later became Genpact, a separate company operating its global headquarters from Gurgaon. Singh dedicated a whole chapter in his autobiography on how Welch was brought to India for doing business.[35]

Having begun his career as a civil engineer in GE, Welch became its chairman and CEO and piloted the company to be a global leader. Singh was introduced to him by a mutual friend and, when Welch visited India, welcomed him with exuberance and pomp. The role of the techno-intellectual troika of Sam Pitroda, chief technology advisor to Prime Minister Rajiv Gandhi, Jairam Ramesh from the Planning Commission and Montek Singh Ahluwalia, special secretary to the prime minister, was vital in managing Welch's visit, which ultimately pioneered the extension of a global business footprint in India. Singh provided details of key meetings on that very important visit and how everything unfolded—a very engrossing story indeed.

At a breakfast meeting organized by Singh in Delhi between Welch and the three-member team, Pitroda made a strong presentation on future business opportunities and directions in India, in which he underlined the business process outsourcing (BPO) prospects, in particular. Welch was highly impressed by the vibrancy of the idea and vision, and reportedly, agreed to invest $10 million to shift a part of GE's outsourcing to India. That marked the second making of Gurgaon, after the advent of Maruti had begun the first one almost two decades earlier.

In the early 1990s, GE started to offload their software work to India and, in 1997, they opened a separate unit in DLF Corporate Park. That very building complex became an iconic point to mark the entry to Gurgaon. GE was soon followed by multinationals like IBM, American Express and British Airways, among others. They opened outsourcing offices, kick-starting the BPO business in India by the end of the last millennium. The period of from 2000 to 2002, known as the Gold Rush period for BPOs, saw many companies opening customer support and telemarketing services. The dot-com was being replaced by the demand for voice-based services, fuelling the flourishing of call centres.

During the 1980s and 90s, Gurgaon had been a residential and industrial suburb, before becoming a place for IT and BPO-driven businesses. Private developers like DLF had already stopped making housing in Delhi. Problems related to unauthorized constructions and incompatible land use simmered in the capital city during the first decade of the millennium. Many big businesses, corporate houses, small- and medium-sized professionals started shifting their work to Gurgaon and other areas of NCR. Developers, both big and small, felt that Delhi would come under pressure soon. The Special Economic Zone (SEZ) Act came into effect in 2005 and Haryana was the first state to enact a matching state-level legislation, resulting in about 40 SEZ projects in Gurgaon alone.

Even in the Development Plan of 2021 and that of 2025, a large area had been earmarked for setting up SEZs. Later, in 2012, the government realized that there were no takers for SEZs and several such notified economic zones were ultimately not implemented. The landowners, too, demanded the re-planning of their land. To address these issues, revisions were initiated in the Final Development Plan of 2025.

To go back to the initial years of development, business parks were set up with high quality infrastructure, similar to the standards of the global corporate sector. The state government also offered preferential treatment for the allotment of land to IT industries in all the industrial areas developed by state agencies. Liberal procedures were practised to change land use, allowing the IT industry and IT parks to locate offices there. Large floor plates in Gurgaon office blocks, with certain building form and type, offered operational flexibility, facilitating corporates to modify the scale of their establishment size easily, to accommodate the wax and wane of the global economy.

Such a business drive initiated a pattern of migration. Blue-collared jobs in the industrial sector were replaced by white-collared employment in service sectors. Job-seekers, then, changed their traditional destinations of industrial and manufacturing-based cities. From Kanpur, Kolkata or Howrah in the colonial days, to Durgapur and Bhilai in the post-independence times, there was a paradigm shift towards IT-based, consultancy-oriented services and related service sector opportunities in Delhi and Gurgaon. The focus and hub of economic activities, too, shifted accordingly.

In search of jobs, low-skilled people from rural Bihar or UP no longer moved to Kolkata in large numbers, which had been their preferred destination for the last couple of centuries. Mumbai and the NCR started offering them new hope, and Gurgaon, a late entrant in this list, became a place of greener pastures. The growth of business in the NCR during the post-liberalization decades and the availability of a large educated population, encouraged call centres and BPOs to locate their offices in Gurgaon. As a job destination, this area gradually became increasingly attractive, encouraging more and more migration.

Nowadays, whenever I take a radio-taxi, I usually start a conversation with the driver. Almost eight out of ten turn out to be from Bihar. A couple of them have been from UP. I came across only one driver each from Rajasthan and Himachal Pradesh. The man from Rajasthan was a Brahmin, but he had not studied much. It was difficult for him to take up a job in his locality, which was not really 'respectable' for his lineage. So, he left his home and came to Delhi and joined one of the radio-taxi services. The stories of the drivers from Bihar are similar—absence of opportunities in agriculture and industry meant that there was hardly any work for them in their native places. Interestingly, one person was a double migrant—his parents had shifted base from Bihar to Kolkata-Howrah and worked in the industry there. Having done a driver's job in Kolkata for some years, he finally shifted to Delhi. Such migrant drivers often found employment in Gurgaon, a place for BPO and call centre services with late working hours, especially before the introduction of different types and brands of radio-taxi services.

Besides IT-based sectors, top consultancy organizations like McKinsey, Deloitte, PwC, Ernst & Young and KPMG have their offices in Gurgaon. In the mid-1990s, McKinsey had their office in Taj Mahal Hotel in Lutyens' Delhi; PwC operated from Delhi for a long time. Over the years, these leading companies shifted their base from Delhi to Gurgaon and having followed their footsteps, the next line of consultancy companies, too, moved their offices to Gurgaon. The city has become the hub of mainstream consultancy business today. It has also become a place for a number of international multi-disciplinary architectural offices that began India operations.

Over and above, the 'sealing drive' in Delhi in the middle of the first decade of the millennium prompted many other smaller professional consultancy offices to relocate their base to Gurgaon. Many of these firms operating from residential areas in Delhi anticipated legal problems and, in a knee-jerk reaction, moved out. Amidst the IT sector's inseparable association with the city, the consultancy business cluster here has rarely received much recognition.

Another related sector comprising EPC (Engineering, Procurement and Construction) companies is not often linked to Gurgaon, though the city has gradually become the hub of such operations, with Bechtel and Flour Daniel, both from USA, Lurgi of Germany, ABB of Switzerland and others setting up their offices in the region. The aphorism that 'almost every major power plant project in the world would have at least one part of it designed in the region' underlines the omnipresence and dominance of these players situated in the NCR belt.[36] Of late, a number of engineer friends, however, do complain that the business has shrunk for a while and multiple cost-cutting measures including issuance of 'pink slips' to employees are being undertaken by some of these companies.

Tathagata Chatterji, an urban designer and planner, cited the story of Siemens to accentuate the importance of this city as a global location in the EPC sector.[37] Siemens, a pioneer in sourcing engineering and manufacturing solutions in India since the 1920s, set up a global competence centre for designing thermal plants in Gurgaon in the late 1990s, almost after 70 years of its operation. Siemens Power Engineering Pvt. Ltd. (SPEL) started with 40 engineers and by 2015, employed 600 engineers—an almost 15 times growth in key personnel. The centre provides 'plant layout engineering' for all EPC projects by Siemens Power Generation. When the company planned to move from Kuala Lumpur to India, there were few location options upfront—Mumbai, Bengaluru, Kolkata and Delhi NCR. Siemens India had its head office in Mumbai, but the city was found to be too expensive for housing. Bengaluru being the head office for Siemens Information Systems could have been a choice. However, the company felt that it would be difficult to find personnel with a power engineering background in that region. Delhi and Kolkata, which had companies like National Thermal Power Corporation (NTPC), Bharat Heavy Electricals Limited (BHEL) and Development Consultants Limited (DCL), with experts in power plant design, became shortlisted locations for the company. The final choice was narrowed down to the NCR, a thriving urban agglomeration, as opposed to Kolkata, a city in economic stagnation. Top managers from NTPC and BHEL and junior level engineers from DCL preferred Delhi because they could foresee opportunities and growth for themselves, good education for their children and a comfortable lifestyle for the family. To such a group of upwardly mobile professionals, Gurgaon was supposedly offering the most 'premium lifestyle' in northern India and it became the preferred office location.

This propensity of choosing Gurgaon as the 'new' working place has been exhibited by many other businesses. With growing numbers of shopping malls, five-star hotels, golf courses, business parks, Fortune 500 companies and elite apartment blocks, the city has become concomitant with an imagined living 'style' (which may not be the same as living 'condition') for the educated service sector personnel. It will be interesting to find out the area of shopping mall per 1,000 persons here and compare that with other cities. Qualified individuals from management, IT and engineering disciplines from various parts of the country have, over the years, found Gurgaon their work place, or 'karmabhumi'.

⁂

Being a part of a larger urban agglomeration also helped Gurgaon a lot, as it could offer greater opportunities and facilitate upward social mobility. Ambition has always been nurtured within the opportunities offered here and is encouraged because Gurgaon has been a part of the larger urban system.

An urban agglomeration is a contiguous urban area formed by a city or a town with outgrowths attached, or by a city and adjoining towns with their outgrowths, if any. Railway colonies, university campuses, port area, military camps and similar settlements next to a city or a town and in continuation with it, are known as outgrowths. Gurgaon, Noida and Ghaziabad, being next to the mega-city of Delhi, form such an agglomeration. Besides that, the Regional Plan 2021 for the NCR identifies nine districts in Haryana, including Gurgaon, within the Haryana sub-region. Gurgaon is not only an agglomeration, but also a part of the Capital Region.

In 1901, the urban population of Gurgaon was less than 5,000 and after independence, in 1951, it went up to a little less than 20,000, with a growth rate of almost 90 per cent. During 1951–61, the population doubled. Gurgaon grew from a class III town in 1970 to a city of about 90,000 people in 1981. With a steady growth rate in 1991 and 2001, the urban population went up to about 1.2 lakh and 2.0 lakh respectively. By 2011, Gurgaon's urban population increased over 8.9 lakh. Besides a tremendous influx of people, the increase in the urban area of Gurgaon contributed to the sharp growth. The first decade of the millennium witnessed a phenomenal growth, the fastest in the NCR. The first half of that particular decade, perhaps, saw the best time of Gurgaon, drawing upon the advantage of being a part of an urban agglomeration. In effect, the attractiveness of the city in a particular sector pulls more businesses and people to the place.

An online news report by *Livemint* in 2014 suggested that till that time, the licence for about 17,000 acres had been given to over 340 developers.[38] The arrival of newer developers increased during the tenure of the last state government, but the three initial entrants, DLF, Ansals and Unitech, still accounted for about 38 per cent of the area, the report suggested. Each of the three big developers tried to build an exclusive pocket of presence: DLF in north-east and east Gurgaon, Ansals in the north-west and Unitech in the centre. Interestingly, the maximum licence allotment happened in 2008, when the world economy faced a 'credit

Ambition

crisis' and the real estate sector in India was hit very badly. Despite being cash-starved and facing low response from buyers, builders made speculative purchases of land and ended up with unfinished projects for a long time. At one point, Golf Course Road used to look like a site of unfinished projects, with cranes stranded and no workers or construction activities. It seemed like a magic wand had stopped everything there.

In such circumstances, in mid-November 2012, the Town and Country Planning Department of the Haryana government revised the Final Development Plan of 2025, which had been notified in May 2011.[39] The perspective period for the plan was extended to 2031. To accommodate the projected population of 42.50 lakh at the end of 2031, almost 40,000 acres (16,021 hectares) of land have been reserved for residential use. Within that area, about 20,000 acres (8,000 hectares) of residential land has already been developed by HUDA and the private 'colonizers', and is expected to house about 20 lakh people. The existing town and villages within the urbanized area, too, accommodate around a population of 2 lakh. The additional residential area would cater to the rest of the population of 20.5 lakh.

By the second decade of the millennium, Gurgaon had about 26 shopping malls, seven golf courses, luxury shops with Chanel and Louis Vuitton products, car showrooms selling Mercedes Benz, BMW and Audi, and the Cyber City commercial precinct housing most of the top offices in the world, according to a story in *The New York Times*, which furnished such a list while discussing the pros and cons of Gurgaon.[40]

I was curious to know about the recent price of Chanel bags, and found out that a lower-end small flap bag would cost close to ₹2 lakh or more! No wonder, the city was considered to be one of the fastest growing districts in the country, a source of almost half of all revenue for Haryana, and added about 50,000 vehicles annually to the roads—a place of high glamour quotient with shine and gloss![41] Gurgaon's real estate had been at its peak at that time, which would soon slump and stagnate because of the combined effects of recession, inflation and scandals. In 2010–11, when I was frequenting Gurgaon almost every day, despite having been the busiest construction arena a few years back, the place used to bear a deserted look with stationary cranes adorning the skyline.

Till the arrival of the Metro and the Rapid Metro, the city could not boast of any public transport. The Metro helped to connect the city with its big brother, Delhi. Otherwise, Gurgaon has more cars than two wheelers on the road, which is itself an amazing feature, completely defying the norms of other Indian cities. In other words, the lower middle class are yet to find their foothold in the city.

Privatization and individual convenience are at its prime display in Gurgaon. Companies employ hundreds of private buses and taxis. Big BPO offices have their own private fleet of vehicles for independent pick-up and drop-off services without any reliance on the conspicuously missing public transport. For social interaction and recreation, residential enclaves have their own clubs, swimming pools, gymnasiums and related facilities.

Since security is a burning issue in Gurgaon like in many other cities, the city has almost four times as many private security guards as police officers. Private developers have their own private police-like personnel in place as well. DLF, for example, has recently constituted its own 'Quick Response Team' or the QRT, a group of men in black dress patrolling DLF territory on motorbikes.[42]

To mitigate the rampant power cuts of Gurgaon, residential and commercial areas have their own generator sets ensuring uninterrupted power supply. The humming of the generators, and at times even the smoke spiralling out of its diesel engine, coupled with the smell, have become a part and parcel of Gurgaon's environment. Scarcity of water has been met by digging private bore-wells and purchasing drinking water. Various reports suggest that Gurgaon's water table depleted alarmingly during the years of its urbanization: from a depth of 6.64 metres in 1974, it went down almost four times to 26.88 metres in 2018.[43] The steady diminution of the groundwater level is another telling impression being left for the future generations to alleviate. A number of NGOs and citizen groups are now actively working on the issue of water in Gurgaon.

The city has evolved a counter-mechanism to deal with the complete 'ad hocism' of the severe lack of governmental provision for basic services, as well as the absence of urban planning. Gurgaon demonstrates how a 'weakness', created due to no support from the government in providing certain basic services, can be turned around as the 'strength', in order to sell the idea of exclusive comfort. In turn, Gurgaon has become another kind of agglomeration of enclaves always trying to be self-sufficient and enhancing the level of self-comfort without batting an eyelid at the sordid impact on natural resources and issues of sustainability.

'I think Gurgaon's social life is thrice more hectic than Delhi's. Here, everyone is super-social—young, energetic and eager to project an image,' a friend from one of the DLF colonies said to me once. People get out of their enclaves, board their luxury cars, go to the glitzy destinations, interact over there, and come back home—this is the familiar cycle of activity. Most of the people in Gurgaon easily associate themselves with something glamorous and visible, which is why its public spaces are 'imagined' sites of abundance underlining the culture of consumption and their corresponding domestic realms reflect a similar desire for a lavish lifestyle.

Gurgaon being a small city, has a limited social circle, spread over its finite space. Most of the children from similar backgrounds go to the same school. Perhaps it helps them socialize more easily than their parents, who could not interact much after school hours, since they lived and studied in Delhi, a much larger city. Even today, it is difficult for school going children in Delhi to have extensive social exchanges with their classmates who stay far away.

Gurgaon's modest spatial scale is suitable for interactions after school hours as well. Parents of school-going children are familiar with each other as they tend to meet socially or professionally in Gurgaon. However, it is important to note that social exchanges, too, have changed their dimensions in the digital networking era! Yet, the global pandemic has shown how much we miss the face-to-face interactions, which otherwise was taken for granted, in our daily lives.

Having spoken to many residents, each time I sense their strong association with the city, perhaps accentuated by its scale and a perceived acquaintance with it. A resident, who has been involved in many city-specific voluntary activities, said, 'As human beings, we want our city to improve and that is why we are involved in social activities, to bring about changes for a better city.'

Technology undoubtedly encourages more jobs, but at the expense of a labour force that tends to become highly stratified. The management-labour power balance thoroughly tilts in favour of the management. The labour force is also flexible enough to fit within the 'just-in-time' (JIT) methodology, popularized by Toyota in the 1960s and 1970s, by reducing the flow-time within production and the response time from the suppliers and customers. In terms of numbers, clerical jobs are in attenuation, resulting in a decline in the number of middle-income households. Gurgaon is essentially 'capitalist', where success is coterminous with the brand of clothes, the car model, the residential address, the corporate office and position of work. The conventional value system is altered in this process.

While simply moving around the roads of Gurgaon, one may notice the apparent existence of polarities of various types: a dhaba within the glitz of corporate offices; malls and tea stalls, squatters and high-end gated enclaves, and so on and so forth. Most of the cities in India may have similar situations, but in Gurgaon, it is perhaps more visible and obvious. As a result, there seems to be a constant scrimmage between the old and new Gurgaon, the modern and the traditional, the rich and the poor, the urban and the rural.

Many such contradictions do happen because of the ambition being pursued by people. Landless labourers flock to the city of Gurgaon in search of work. The success and glamour in the city are right there for them to see. It is both tempting and inspiring for a rustic peasant who has just arrived in a new place to survive. He often comes to the city because some of his village neighbours are here. He sees them doing reasonably well and they tell him interesting stories about city life. He, too, jumps into the fray.

A large number of domestic helps are from the eastern part of the country. Many of them speak Bengali. Whenever I asked them about their native place, they respond with Malda, Dinajpur, Murshidabad or Nadia. These districts in West Bengal are located next to the Indo-Bangladesh border. Their dialects often indicate their Bangladeshi roots. They prefer to choose Gurgaon and the NCR, where more minute observations on their dialect would remain unnoticed and they could easily be identified as Bengalis from West Bengal.

Drivers and security guards come mostly from Bihar, with a few from UP. Construction labours, too, are from the hinterlands of Bihar and Bengal. Having seen the lucrative opportunity in land dealing, many local Haryana people became real estate brokers, a business that requires more muscle power, contacts and 'courage' to handle raw cash as well as to close big money deals. Corporate professionals came from all over the country and usually their social circles cut across religion, ethnicity and caste groups. Their friends are their neighbours, office colleagues or parents of their children's school or college mates. Even during festivals like Durga Puja, everyone tends to participate in a big way. In that sense, the corporate citizens of Gurgaon are pan-Indian with a global desire and aspiration.

No one can deny the bewildering pace at which the city has grown over the years. From nowhere, it has become a corporate hub of about 250 Fortune 500 companies. The frenzied aspirational push of a large population of migrants from across the country drives the city. Ambitious and unrealistic self-targets are set by seeing the world around and not by judging one's own potentials and opportunities. Often, the failure to reach the lofty target makes people dejected and exasperated. When the swell of ambition is not fulfilled in the legitimate way, many even opt for shortcuts. This ambitious quest to capture the shine and glitter of the place may also end up in vicious repercussions.

Interestingly, Gurgaon, of late, has been a backdrop of

crime fiction. I once read a newspaper report on this topic that included some of the popular crime fiction writers in the city and discussed how they find the story within the city itself.[44] Gurgaon has become a prolific location for fictional plots exposing the dark underbelly of an otherwise glossy city.

Gurgaon has never been a conventional Indian city. In fact, it has never tried to be one. Gurgaon is the new social address, although Lutyens' Delhi has remained the number one choice for the rich and the mighty. The person who was credited for the upsurge of Gurgaon, K.P. Singh of DLF, does not live in Gurgaon but in Lutyens' Delhi. The same is true for Sushil Ansal, whose family lives close to Lutyens' Delhi. Having started as a choice for Delhi residents who could not afford to buy a house in south Delhi, Gurgaon afforded a new lifestyle for many, with a different set of facilities offered in the high-rise apartments. Over the years, newer housing projects have come up, with new USPs (Unique Selling Points).

For over a decade, I taught in an architecture college in Gurgaon. In architecture education, the main learning space is called a 'studio' where various architectural design problems are introduced. Gurgaon was central to many of the design problems that I introduced to my students. Once, a housing design problem was introduced to the senior level students for which they had to first conceptualize, select the site of their choice, decide the design brief and finally design the housing project.

Ambition

To begin with, they had to design a poster for their proposed housing. Many of the students were from the NCR and it was interesting to see how most of them aspired to make a housing that was set within nature or imbibed fragments of it. Housing for them was more like a resort, spaced out and huddled within the green. 'Urban Forest', 'Urban Woods', 'Urban Resorts' and 'Urban Oasis' were some of the popular names of their proposed utopian housing exercises. Later, many real housing projects came up in Gurgaon, highlighting similar intentions to project a 'better' quality of life—the X-factor of luxury living that portrays success.

Gurgaon is different from Mumbai or Delhi. If Delhi is a city for the political class and Mumbai for businessmen and film stars, Gurgaon is for professionals. Over the years, it has indeed become a 'karmabhumi' for them. Recently, I met Jyoti Sagar, an eminent lawyer, and his wife, Prema, a top public relations (PR) consultant. Her PR company was founded at the beginning of the 1990s and she has been an important figure in India's PR realm. Around the same time, Jyoti founded his law firm, which has grown to become a top consultancy in India with over three hundred professionals, alongside a booming intellectual property law practice. Eventually, both of them shifted their respective offices to Gurgaon from where their profession grew to new heights. Perhaps, of all the people I have known in the city, Jyoti and Prema have been staying there for the longest period of time.

Gurgaon to Gurugram

In 1991, they built their house behind the Bristol hotel on a piece of land bought in the early 1980s and started settling in Gurgaon. During those days, both of them concurred; it was rare to get visitors at home because their friends from Delhi were so apprehensive of visiting so far in the evening. In fact, they had fixed a high power lamp on a tall pole over the terrace of their house so that visitors to their house could see it from a long distance. And that was how they used to give directions to their place. A city that boasts of signature structures today was then devoid of any identifiable landmark.

Prema, the daughter of an Indian father and a Swiss mother, was brought up in a 'fauji' environment. Once she asked her father about her religion: 'We are military', was her dad's curt response. I found it a fascinating little anecdote that somewhat captured the profile of Gurgaon citizens—cosmopolitan, contemporary and secular. Most of the people here are known for what they do and not for what their lineages are. Gurgaon has given them that space and opportunity to flourish, and they, in turn, have also been involved in significant social and charitable activities, bringing change in their city and society.

From 'the mustard field with a handful of structures here and there', as the Sagars described the initial days of the city, to what we see today, has been a captivating urban journey. The influx of new people with varied aspirations—of career, wealth, comfort and way of living—required a new image of the city. Gurgaon's developers, and in due course, the city at large, have created a unique brand that no other city in India had at that point. In fact, it has been the optics that carried the lasting impression of Gurgaon to everyone's mind.

IMPRESSION

Of the Extraordinary

It was the autumn of 1997. I drove down a gentle slope on MG Road soon after crossing the Delhi-Gurgaon border. The road took a turn to the left, leading towards Sikanderpur. My eyes travelled unencumbered and DLF Corporate Park, with its four glass-and-metal buildings, appeared on the right. That was my first impression of Gurgaon. Today, the Metro causeway and pillars have taken away that visual drama.

At that time, our architecture practice had just received a small interior project in Gurgaon, for an Italian fast food chain that wanted us to design a small outlet. For the same group, we had just concluded a larger sit-out-cum-take-away restaurant in South Extension Part I market in south Delhi. Driving down Gurgaon was like visualizing Bruce Springsteen's 'My Hometown'—perhaps the most uncharacteristic number by the singer! It was an 'interesting' sight with towers popping out of the otherwise barren landscape with a few patches of agricultural land. The urban project of building Gurgaon, I realized, had begun, and it was indeed a 'green-field' development.

Since then, Gurgaon's urbanism has consisted of dots, patches, stretches and parcels, and their manipulation and consolidation. Buildings of different sizes and shapes mark the landscape. Patches of green field coexist with demarcated land parcels bought by developers, alongside the buildings of business parks, housing and shopping malls. Shades of brown of bare plots and parts of the rocky ridge, dashes of green here and there and the grey roads make the background palette.

The skyline on the foreground is formed by colourful, shiny and reflective buildings. In the heat of the scorching summer in the Aravallis, the bougainvillea blooms, a scatter of magenta above the bamboo stubbles of fences around office complexes. On the dusty pavement outside, hawkers wait indolently with cold drinks, nimboo soda and sliced guavas sprinkled with black salt.

'If we look back at 2002–2003, Gurgaon was not seen as a city at that time by the people who started living here. They saw it more like a conclave or a small colony,' a Gurgaon resident says. I think that perception still continues. All the DLF phases are considered to be one colony, more like another Greater Kailash. Gurgaon has not been seen as a city in the making but as an assortment of conclaves that came up one after the other and sometimes together.

Most often, sets of conclaves developed by different real estate giants came up away from each other, thereby creating distinctive identities. Other than the phases of DLF and Sushant Lok by Ansals, Nirvana by Unitech became another conclave of new Gurgaon. These distinguishable enclaves tried to construct a brand identity and lifestyle. At the same time, the concept of the Master Plan as a static document was kept aside. The idea of a 'blueprint city' like Delhi, dictated by an all-pervasive document, was rejected in the methods and tactics of assembling Gurgaon right from the beginning.

Any such document had to be dynamic and evolving and could incorporate the required changes within a short span of time—that has been an unstated fact here. HUDA, many felt, had realized that as the planning agency, their default role was to provide broad guidelines while giving 'freedom' to developers. It may have started as the deviation from the usual planning dogma, but in the long run it allowed some amount of variation and richness to the urban texture of Gurgaon. However, such loosely manipulated planning also created enough infrastructural worry for the city and for its citizens.

In the initial years, Gurgaon was broadly divided into six identifiable urban precincts: old Gurgaon, industrial area, Cyber-Hub, DLF phases and Sushant Lok areas, Nirvana areas and HUDA sectors. Difference has been the essence of the prevailing visual order in Gurgaon. Earlier, one could identify certain striking buildings, but now, for every large building, the design mandate is to make it 'different', at least from the neighbouring ones. This often makes it difficult to distinguish and appreciate the architectural uniqueness of a particular building. It is like hunting for a red ball in a bag full of different coloured balls. If most of the balls were of one or two colours, the red ball being the third colour would stand out. Today, plenty of landmarks are known by their names and not by their visual presence.

While crossing the Delhi-Gurgaon Toll Plaza on the National Highway, one cannot miss the Gateway Tower to the left. It is a ship-like, 12-storey structure spread over 1 acre, with a floor area of about 85,000 sq. ft. To its admirers, it represents 'futuristic architecture'. Its 'dynamic' form, the architect of the building explains, is supposed to function as a gateway to DLF Cyber City, with its curvilinear facade capturing the eye while turning from the highway, its materiality helping it stand out visually.

> [The building has] an aesthetic based on tectonics. The building is sheathed with granite and glass in which the granite dominates the lower levels and the higher levels are totally wrapped in glass. The stone at the lower level responds to the tactile and the glass augments the visual quality for a spectator. Vertically striated stone surfaces enable the curving glass walls, which are horizontally composed, to visually emerge rather than collide.[45]

The tower was the first major building in the Cyber City precinct and today, it is surrounded with a large parking lot. Critics consider the Gateway Tower to be a 'symbol' of the city's private wealth, growing inequality and 'unsustainable' building, and such voices are not few and far between.[46] Interestingly, the façade of this building has been used as a digital advertising hoarding too. That is how image and impression merge in Gurgaon. We also find similar images of urban expansion in Greater Noida, New Town Kolkata, Navi Mumbai and many other relatively recent developments in smaller cities and towns. Even in Jaipur, for example, where heritage is a key ingredient of the city and people at different levels of decision-making are quite aware of its significance, newer architecture follows similar aesthetics, presenting a sense of technological progress to the common eye.

The representation in (and of) Gurgaon is, thus, generic and global. The optics and technics of this brand of image is virological, as it spreads everywhere like a virus and is being infected continuously by an updated one. The original source of any such virus is not clearly known. Cyberspace seems to work like this; messages are circulated without having any idea of the original source and authenticity. Architectural imageries and the corresponding functions of buildings in Gurgaon have sources in Singapore, USA, Spain and elsewhere. Similarly, new constructions in other cities in India have found examples of Gurgaon-type representation as inspirations. This chain of diffusion continues unabated, while taking advantage of highly accessible and transferable images in this era of the Internet.

Conversely, the production of Gurgaon is specific and contextual because of a complex and unique combination of land, productivity, price, law, proximity to Delhi and

Impression

many other sub-factors, as discussed earlier. This gives rise to a couple of questions: Are the impression and image exchangeable? If so, can we understand the image of Gurgaon using established discourses?

The original Latin use of the word 'impression' meant a 'mark produced by pressure' and its French version indicated 'a pressing on the mind'. Symbolically, the word is used for 'mental impression', a perception. At the beginning of the twentieth century, the phrase 'public impression' was used selectively, till it became popular parlance in advertising and public relations in the late 1950s. Image, on the other hand, referred to the imagination or the formation of a mental picture of tangible things.

While impression is about perception, image is about imagination, and in the case of Gurgaon, the prevailing visual construct is an overlap of the two. Therefore, in a city like this, where real buildings and built spaces—as well as their imagined versions—are displayed on advertising hoardings to project a perception of a certain way of living, the subtle modernist ideological difference between image and impression is drowned in a whirlpool of information, advertising and aspiration. In turn, the words become conveniently interchangeable.

Guy Debord, a French philosopher and filmmaker, introduced the idea of 'the commodity as spectacle' in the late 1960s. The spectacle becomes a 'social relationship between people that is mediated by images', that is far beyond the assemblage of images.[47] Reification is a complex concept, Debord discussed, through which immaterial ideas are converted into or represented by material things, like the way a wedding ring represents love or, in a simplistic sense, a developer's brochure projects a certain quality of life.

Artefacts (buildings) and the optics (aesthetics of architecture), both, by being sufficiently visible have transformed themselves into a new mode of communication. 'Image' is a loosely termed notion encapsulating this transformation of an object into communication, and somewhat becomes a hybrid of an object-communication-technology construct. The production of an image, whether in Gurgaon or in other places, quite often tends to fall back on a technological source for inspiration or justification.

The conventional image-construct, relying upon established notions of focus-fabric or figure-ground, may not hold true for understanding the legibility of this place. 'Legibility' is a term popularized by an American urban designer, Kevin Lynch (1918–84) in his significant book, *The Image of the City* (1960). If we cannot make out a scribble on paper, we often say, 'It is not legible.' Lynch imbibed this idea and applied it to the process of way-finding in the city. While moving in a city, if people cannot recognize a coherent pattern, that place is not 'legible'.

In other words, cities can not only be seen and experienced, but also be 'read' with the help of these five elements, which depict the ideas of similarity (districts), orientation (landmarks), destination (nodes), contiguity (paths) and its break (edges).[48] Of these, paths seem to be the key element because of their granularity and contribution to urban mobility. An appropriate interpretation of these elements may help to make visual sense of a place, if not of the city as a whole. Many critics, however, label such ideas as 'western' with very limited applicability in Indian cities. Gurgaon, one should remember, never wished to be an 'Indian city', whatever that may mean.

Urban fabric refers to the physical urban environment comprising of the form of a building, activities, the scale and the arrangement of open spaces between and around buildings and roads, materials used, density of people and buildings, networks of mobility, open spaces and natural features. All these components create the basic imagery of any part of a city. That is why, despite being residential areas, the urban fabric of Lodhi Colony in central Delhi, Greater Kailash in South Delhi and ITC Laburnum in Gurgaon are totally different. The notion of fabric and its texture has been borrowed from cloth and applied to understand a city.

Qualities like similarity, uniformity and consistency can make a fabric, whether it is a cloth or a city. The texture of cotton cloth is different from that of tusser silk; similarly, the urban texture of DLF Phase II is poles apart from that of Chakkarpur, despite being adjacent to each other. The former has planned layouts, wide roads, plotted buildings with garden-yards, whereas the latter has incremental arrangements of buildings, narrow yet active streets, and buildings without gardens but with courtyards, which were later converted to rooms. Different textures give rise to different fabrics, forming the base image layer of a city. Urban fabric is, thus, made out of an 'ordinary' group of buildings representing a certain kind of built environment. 'Ordinary' here means common buildings of any city, for example, buildings along the streets of old Jaipur or Udaipur, or urban blocks in Kolkata, Mumbai or Barcelona, to illustrate only a few.

Urban focus, on the contrary, is formed once a building or a space is easily identifiable because of its difference from the urban fabric surrounding it. Focus is somewhat similar to what is referred to as 'landmark'. Since the image-making of Gurgaon is conceptually based on difference and not on similarity, most of the buildings here have been imagined as focus buildings. As a result, the urban fabric has a very limited physical existence in this place. Therefore, it is not really appropriate to read the legibility of Gurgaon with a focus-fabric construct. This is different from the image-making of Jaipur for example, where the street facades of the walled city area are made to create a uniform look by using the same colour and similar architectural elements—similarity created an image and gave Jaipur the name, 'Pink City'.

Before understanding how we can read a city like Gurgaon, we need to look at the prevailing trends of using architecture as a stylistic statement and its subsequent issues.

'Elegant, extravagant, flashy, dazzling. The new corporate architecture is changing the way Indian suburbia looks' is how an article in 2002 in *The Indian Express* described what

Impression

Gurgaon wanted to be, and it was a conscious shift from the notion of conventional suburbs.[49] Very often, architectural styles and the stylized names of built projects like Malibu Town, Signature Tower, Princeton, Aralia, or Belvedere Park are used as tools to stand out as landmark projects, outsmart competitors and repackage products to attract consumers. The purpose is to create an impression and tap into an aspirational lifestyle. This is the way in which the culture of the production and consumption of an image has now taken over the social space as well.

Fredric Jameson, a leading critical theorist, wrote a series of articles in the 1980s and 90s addressing the cultural, social and market economy-driven nuances of the consumerist time he lived in.[50] Although time has surpassed some of his key points, yet quite a few are relevant in helping us realize why the imagery of Gurgaon is what it is. One stylistic feature of postmodern art and architecture, he considers, is *pastiche*—a way of 'mimicry of other styles and particularly of mannerisms and stylistic twitches of other styles'. This is applicable to the description of a large number of architecture in Gurgaon, trapped within mimicry and replication, borrowing images from somewhere else to rekindle the aspiration of people.[51] Some Spanish villas or a tower in Singapore that a developer liked on his last family trip become the inspiration for his project in Gurgaon. When he wants that to be replicated here, to imitate pre-existing styles would be the only option left. 'Stylistic innovation' would no longer be possible. Instead, pastiche prevails.

Gurgaon to Gurugram

> [I]n this new stage the very sphere of culture itself has expanded, becoming coterminous with market society in such a way that the culture is no longer limited to its earlier, traditional or experimental forms, but is consumed throughout daily life itself, in shopping, in professional activities, in the various often televisual forms of leisure, in production for the market and in the consumption of those market products, indeed in the secret folds and corners of the quotidian.[52]

Jameson talks about a certain kind of architecture creating showpieces of past styles and in turn, converting a city to another kind of museum. In a city like Gurgaon, it goes one step further. It becomes a 'kingdom of dreams', a post-informational museum exhibiting an impression of life seen in Hollywood films and on foreign trips, and most importantly, making it available to all of us right here in the backyard of India's capital. Indeed, the city has become a destination since the mid-1990s for engineers, managers and professionals, all aspiring to fulfil the dreams of a certain kind of lifestyle.

In the 1970s, Delhi had its own Pragati Maidan, literally the 'Ground of Progress', to display the achievement and coherent endeavours of the country. Pavilions supposedly representing the different states of India and other departmental pavilions were erected. As a whole, it was a heterogeneous mix of another kind, a 'Nation of Dreams', albeit under an overarching ideological canopy of the Centre-state. Not surprisingly, in a zest to rewrite history, landmark structures of Pragati Maidan were demolished in 2017 for redevelopment, replacing the iconic buildings with a state-of-the-art exhibition space, apparently in a bid to 'modernize' the venue.

On the other hand, Gurgaon has its own quasi-indoor air-conditioned 'Kingdom of Dreams', arranged in an eclectic manner with replicas of landmarks from different parts of the country and outside. It is like a gallery of collection and remaking of architectural artefacts. Remake is an interesting trend these days, especially in Hindi films and their music. Reproduction and repackaging of story and song have been a fecund source of imitation. To commentators of postmodernism, Kingdom of Dreams is symptomatic of such trends. It boasts of some scintillating performances. One of the most popular among them is 'Zangoora,' a fantasy story of good versus evil and a love triangle set in a fictional setting. It is an unreal larger-than-life musical, borrowing elements from Bollywood masala movies. Another performance named 'Jhumroo,' coined after an immortal song of Kishore Kumar, is a musical comedy centred around songs from Hindi films and presented with stunning visuals on a breathtaking set. Their magical dreamlike presentations are something that the audience has never seen before, and no other place than Gurgaon could have been a more appropriate venue for these dramas.

Today, Gurgaon's image is that of a larger dream—of ways of working, doing business and living. Earlier, people used to refer to Mumbai as the 'Sapno ka Shahar', the City of Dreams. In that sense, Gurgaon is a mega-sized kingdom of dreams, full of private estates selling dreams. Gurgaon's impression is thus created out of dreams of luxury, style, abundance and flamboyance.

The Spirit of the Age, here, is formed from a paradox: on one side, innovation of technology and communication, with a whole genre of apps marking a new way of life, and on the other side, image-making and its narrative falling back on either certain types of established precedence elsewhere, or churning out something for the sake of making a difference. The architecture of the buildings of Gurgaon, in fact, has added to this potion of urban impression. The identity-making process 'operates across the difference by differing and deferring', and in the context of the architecture of Gurgaon, in terms of both 'time' and 'space'.[53]

In a recent seminar, I heard someone commenting that any urban development brochure of the government carries pictures of roads, bridges and flyovers. In other words, infrastructure becomes the selling point for the developmental agenda of the government. On the contrary, Gurgaon pioneered the act of bringing architecture within the focus of development, even if only for the purpose of representation. This process, of surpassing precedence and adjacency, to a large extent, has failed to achieve the latent objective when instead of the 'excellence' of individual buildings, the collective impression of the city is usually discussed, along with their related cause and effect.

Impression

At the formative stage, certain 'smart' moves were in play in territorializing Gurgaon. This was not aimed at defence or at class-segregation, but to construct imagery and, in turn, allure people to come and settle in Gurgaon. For a green-field development, it is important to capture its limit by marking the entry. For Gurgaon, entries from Delhi were considered important, which made sense.

The transition from Delhi was celebrated and the physical extent of Gurgaon was marked by locating 'signature' buildings with different architectural styles not seen before in the NCR. These were DLF Corporate Park on MG Road, DLF Square with the Gateway Tower on the National Highway and the British Airways building at the Delhi-Faridabad entry. Many of the people I spoke to, felt that these buildings were 'super glamorous' and announced a dramatic change in architectural style at the turn of the millennium. Architecture, like never before, was used for projecting Gurgaon as a future destination. Today, Gurgaon and many other cities can be accessed by railway or through an airport. In fact, for most of Gurgaon's flamboyant residents, the airport is the biggest gateway to the city.

In contrast, traditional cities were bound by walls and gates, like Old Delhi, Jaipur and many others. Colonial cities used different tools for defining their territory, often using railway lines and/or open green spaces. The question of access to the city has to be asked in a new way: does the city have a façade? The popular expression, 'go into city', has to be replaced by 'go to the city', as we are never in front of the city but within it.

The urban order, geometry and axiality found in cities in India during medieval and colonial times have been disregarded in contemporary cities. The artistic forms of cities are no longer a source of inspiration. Many commentators identify suburbia as the sole culprit for the dilution of city and countryside relationships. Gurgaon is like a part of a mega-city now. On my first visit to Gurgaon, discussed at the beginning of this chapter, I had felt a sense of entry to the place, which has now disappeared.

Over time, a celebrated entry into the walled city would lose its prominence as the city extended outside its walls. For example, in Jaipur, which I frequented in recent times due to work, the existence of the old city is hardly distinguishable till one enters it through the gate. On the main streets of the walled city area, geometry, grid, grand city level axis and urban elements, all coalesce. Over the years, the gates and the city wall in Jaipur have been suffocated by parking, encroachment and insensitive development. To walk along the wall would be a challenging and virtually impossible task. Outside the walled city, images are, by now, quite similar to most of the other cities in India.

Postcolonial cities are, by and large, marred by the functional zoning and the land use plan borrowed from the North American planning repository. Delhi, the precursor, adopted the Master Plan-based urban planning, along the same line of thinking. However, in the architecture of buildings, there had been a certain transition from an

Impression

'International Style' to a quest for Indian versions. In this respect, Gurgaon is different. Planning here has long faded out. Hence, there has hardly been any opportunity to clutch onto the imported version of urban planning. However, the architecture of buildings has been highly influenced by anything that was not present elsewhere in the country. Gurgaon is a post-planning city and, at the same time, an example of the pre-infrastructure city.

⚘

A couple of Gurgaon residents have an interesting point to make. The high-end housing delivery, they feel, has hit a barrier. If the price of a flat in Gurgaon goes beyond ₹10 crore of rupees, it becomes difficult for the builder to sell it. The prospective owners of such flats, it appears, prefer Delhi. At the same time, it has become difficult for developers, too, to come up with an exclusive brand of 'luxury' housing without raising the cost a lot. Some of them, however, have taken a risk and delivered a few super-luxury housing, but that may be seen as an exception and not a generic trend. In this context, affordable housing is coming up to fill the void. A little less than 50 licenses have been issued for over 230 acres of land to be developed as 'affordable housing'.

With this type of housing delivery, upcoming projects in Gurgaon got another dimension. Affordability has become the focus of advertising campaigns, in tune with the central government's National Mission for Urban Housing initiative, to provide housing under the slogan of 'Housing for All by 2022'. The previous United Progressive Alliance (UPA) government had schemes like Jawaharlal Nehru National Urban Renewal Mission (JNNURM) and Rajiv Awas Yojana (RAY), which were merged with the present National Democratic Alliance (NDA) government's 'Pradhan Mantri Awas Yojana (Urban)–Housing for All' in June 2015. Besides extremely high-end apartments and penthouses, several developers are targeting middle-income groups through affordable housing. The erstwhile developers, so far, have tucked themselves away from this particular real estate portfolio, which opened up business spaces for another set of entrants to deliver.

In October 2017, the Haryana state cabinet removed the cap on land for affordable housing. Instead of 10 acres per sector, it has become 15 acres and effectively, the 300 acres cap for the total land for affordable housing for Gurgaon has also been removed. Over 35,000 housing units are reported to be under construction in Gurgaon, and another 24,000 units may come up if time-bound clearance of licences is ensured and if timely allotment of licences is attended to.[54] The majority of these projects are located in the newer sectors, under either the Gurgaon-Manesar Urban Complex 2031 or the Sohna Urban Development Plan.

Once developed, affordable housing shall bring another dimension to urban morphology and its resultant imagery. Gurgaon, once at the periphery of Delhi, will eventually have its own outskirts, away from the original main city.

Impression

Many professionals settled in Gurgaon in the mid-1990s at a formative stage of their career. Most of them had grown up in different parts of Delhi and had some level of familiarity with various services and activities there. They continued working in Delhi and sent their children to schools there. Some of them even procured their groceries from previously known stores in the capital. In fact, Gurgaon truly worked like a suburb then. Initially, they were settlers and slowly became residents of Gurgaon. Over time, the city acquired its next generation, who studied and later began working in Gurgaon. The socio-economic dependence on the big city started evaporating in the last decade. Now, with new locational relationships being drawn up, Gurgaon's morphological allegiance to Delhi is under modification.

This reminds me of what Pramod Bhasin shared, 'New Delhi is fast becoming a suburb of Gurgaon but of course it will take a while before they realize it!' Bhasin, former CEO of Genpact, observed the city closely since the beginning. Time will tell how profound it is, but I find it a very interesting observation in this context.

Gurgaon, especially its imagery, is mostly associated with its newer parts, along arterial roads like the National Highway, MG Road, Cyber City Road, Golf Course Road and Golf Course Extension Road. However, a large part, including Old Gurgaon and areas developed by HUDA, are not part of the popular image of the city. Areas adjoining the Delhi border captivated the notion of Gurgaon at first glance—'pehli nazar', to appropriate a phrase from old Hindi films. This unique urban tactic, embedded in the branding of the upcoming city, was different from many other prevailing notions of image-making and city-building.

As one approached from Delhi, the high-end enclaves and office towers of Gurgaon gleamed, and the villages of Sikanderpur, Nathupur and Chakkarpur are tucked away in the distance. Two broad socially disparate groups existed, each with its respective representations, leaving no room for a middle-income group. However, the imminent expansion to accommodate affordable housing units will create a belt of middle- and lower middle-income groups.

In most cities, one can identify some kind of centre of the city. Despite the Master Plan's attempt to make Delhi a multi-nuclear city, Connaught Place and India Gate continue to form the centre. In that sense, Edwin Lutyens effectively shifted the focus from Shahjahanabad's Red Fort-Chandni Chowk node. The adoption of Lutyens' Delhi as the seat of the capital of post-independence India later boosted its urban centrality. Conventional discourses of centre-periphery hold certain relevance in most cities.

Does centre-periphery interpretation work in Gurgaon? Where is the centre of Gurgaon?

Gurgaon does not have a conventionally identifiable centre. Instead, the city has had shifting centres, as it has grown over the years. Earlier, the centre was the old Gurgaon area, followed by the Maruti factory area. Mehrauli- Gurgaon Road, Cyber City and Golf Course Road followed thereafter. In recent times, development along the newer roads has made those stretches the 'happening places'. As Gurgaon kept on shifting its focus, multiple centres became popular.

The old parts of Gurgaon present a different place altogether. While exploring that part of the city, I looked for 'Kaman Sarai', a wayside inn which, some thought, was an officers' mess. On the way, I asked many people about its whereabouts, but no one could provide proper information. No wonder, in a city that has never bothered about its history, one would not easily recognize such a remnant of the past!

After crossing National Highway, I continued on MG Road till it joined the trishul-like junction popularly referred to as Fountain Chowk. It seemed to mark the beginning of the colonial part of the city. The Old-Delhi-Gurgaon Road is the other important thoroughfare at that crossing. The third is the Bus Stand Road, a connecting street that heads towards the centre of the old city from its northern side via the bus terminus.

A number of sarai, roadside inns in medieval times, like Yusuf Sarai, Katwaria Sarai, Jia Sarai, Ber Sarai and others, used to be found on the road leading to Mehrauli. The distance between Shahjahanabad, popularly known as Old Delhi and Mehrauli, the first seat of the Sultanate, was considered long during those days. The route eventually connected two extremely revered spiritual places, the Dargah of Khwaja Moinuddin Chishti in Ajmer and that of Nizamuddin Chisti in Delhi. Many devotees traversed this road and availed the services offered by the sarai located along it.

Kaman Sarai was one such roadside inn, which lies in obscurity today. Surprisingly, even when we were next to the entry to the sarai, correct directions were not easy to get. Like many other smaller towns in India's hinterland, Gurgaon, too, has been quick to forget its past. Although it has a low concentration of built heritage in comparison to nearby small towns like Rewari, Bawal or Farrukhnagar, whatever little historic structures it had at one point of time, have been either forgotten or are in complete shambles. One sad story is that of a piao, a historic well on MG Road near DLF Corporate Park, which was demolished with the advent of the metro to the city. Today, the Dronacharya station stands on that site.

The name Kaman Sarai, some may think, might have originated from Caravan Sarai. Kaman could also be a vernacular translation of cannon. It could also be related to a garrison that the British set up in Gurgaon after the battle of 1857. On my visit, I missed the stone plaque that had been inscribed at the time of its construction. Later, I was introduced to Dr Rajendra Yadav, a former teacher at a senior secondary school in Gurgaon. Dr Yadav has been a keen observer of the history of the city. Both of us exchanged notes on the sarai. The next day, he returned to the site and sent me an image of the stone plaque. It was a white marble slab and the letters were chiselled onto it and painted black. Over the years, the black paint of the letters has worn off, making the inscriptions less legible. The plaque had the following self-explanatory inscription:

Impression

Zamindars Rest House
Built in May 1925
By R.S. Danpat Rai, Tehsildar, Gurgaon
From Subscriptions
Raised By Lala Shib Shankar, Revenue Assistant
Among the Zamindars of the District
In Honour of Thomas Lugard Brayne
First Son of
Mr. F.L. Brayne, M.C., I.C.S.
Deputy Commissioner of Gurgaon
Born on June 20, 1921

Kaman Sarai, as evident from the plaque, was built to commemorate the birthday of a British officer's son. The sarai was actually meant for local zamindars. Perhaps when they used to visit the British officers in Gurgaon, they stayed here during the day or overnight. The dilapidated arched gate reminded me of its stylistic similarity with the architecture of the late Mughal times. The architectural style, interestingly, did not blindly follow the then prevailing colonial architecture. A set of four arches adorned the gateway. I saw an antique-looking printing press operating from a tiny space within the gate structure. Peepal saplings sprouted from the visible cracks in the structure. Dangling wires crisscrossed the elevation of the gate. Broken plasterwork exposed the underlying brickwork. The structure must have been last painted a very long time ago! The gate, I thought, had borne the brunt of time and was waiting precariously for its eventuality, unless proper conservation work happens soon.

As one entered through the gate, on the left side, was a long barrack-type structure adapted into a police station and a political party's office. The gate directed to a large open space, which was used as a parking. The scale of the space was huge. It was heartbreaking to see the miserable state of what could be a historical landmark in Gurgaon. The place, I thought, would be an apt one to undertake heritage conservation and a renewal project to infuse new activities by reusing the structure. A wonderful public place could be made there.

Of late, increasing infatuation for mythological mystique has been all around, whether in Gurgaon or elsewhere in the country. In fact, the new name of Gurgaon has been given along similar lines. However, the historicity of a place is found unattended in this vein of thought. The eloquence of a mythological narrative often becomes mute in recognizing appropriate historical traces.

Fountain Chowk near the Kaman Sarai was crowded and chaotic. The place looked like a typical medium-sized town, where the population had boomed suddenly. The vibrancy of life was everywhere, with hawkers selling almost everything under the sun. The spicy smell of chhole kulche and bhatura prepared on the roadside food carts attracted a lunchtime crowd waiting for their order to be served. Autos were parked on the road, looking for passengers. People stood, waited and loitered. Most of them had nothing to do with

Impression

the city. They were visitors to the city like me, I realized.

A few new buildings had a bit of glitz, trying to emulate the new Gurgaon imagery. There were a number of ambiguous greyish badly-maintained commercial buildings. I spotted an insignificant-looking gate to a government secondary school behind me and entered to find out more about the area, in case anyone knew more about it.

It was a pleasant surprise! The school building consisted of a set of single-storeyed structures spread on both sides of the entrance. On the right side was a veranda with a series of arches, through which the classrooms could be accessed. The classrooms had windows opening on to the large, centrally located playground of the school. It was a very nicely crafted brick structure from colonial times.

The principal was extremely cordial and helpful. 'A newspaper report indicated that the school site may be taken up by the hospital next door,' she said. If that were to happen, the beautiful school building would be destroyed by newer non-responsive interventions. From the way the corridor and the rooms were arranged, the shape appeared to be an incomplete hexagon with only three remaining sides. Later, I saw the aerial view of the site and the plan-form seemed to be in conjunction with the geometry of adjoining roads. The school, I was told, had been known as the Coronation School in the pre-independence days and, perhaps, was one of the schools established to commemorate the coronation of Prince Edward. Once I read up on the history a little more, I found out some interesting stories. Edward VIII was the King of United Kingdom and Dominions of the British Empire, and the Emperor of India, from January to December 1936. In that case, the school must have been made around that time.

'In probably the leafiest and quietest corner of Old Gurgaon, a little away from the traffic bustle, there stands a comforting monument to history. This is the Church of the Epiphany, which is observing 150 years this year,' a report in the *Times of India*'s Gurgaon edition wrote in 2016.[55] A little way off from the school, situated in Gurgaon's Civil Lines, the old place of worship had a rustic chapel-like scale and ambience. Coloured in brick red, the structure had three distinctive parts of eclectic nature. The first part had three arched openings with a sloping projection over it. This was the entry to the church. The middle portion was a triangular part with a big cross on it. This part continued to become the main assembly hall with the gable roof on top, supported by magnificent wooden beams. The topmost portion was a slender bell tower-like pinnacle.

The church was built by the British government in 1862 and was a place of worship for British officers in town. The government maintained the church in its initial years before handing it over to society. In the initial years, it was under the Diocese of Lahore and from 1970 onwards, became part of the Diocese of Delhi. A recent church building was erected adjacent to the old one to accommodate the growing congregation. When lit up for Christmas celebrations, the old structure is a sight of resplendent glory. The Church marked the post-1857 period, when the British stationed a garrison in Gurgaon.

The shopping malls, corporate offices and high-end gated enclaves somehow stand out when one talks about Gurgaon's imagery. Beside such overwhelming representations of a shining 'global' architectural expression, Gurgaon's villages have existed along with the old part of the city, but both have remained almost as footnotes to the main story. Such contradictions have continued to create a paradoxical nature of the city. Dichotomies are always found in Indian cities, and Gurgaon is no exception.

CONTRADICTION

Between the Ways of Life

Arjun, a small-time contractor, started working in 2016 at one of our project sites in Gurgaon. A middle-aged man, he looks like a hard-working type. He was initially a sub-contractor and eventually took over a part of the execution work in his own capacity. It was a summer morning; he had come to our office to submit some bills.

While talking to him, I got to know that he stayed in Chakkarpur. Since migrating to Gurgaon in 2003, he had been staying in Chakkarpur. He hailed from a family of farmers from Chhattarpur village in Madhya Pradesh, about 135 km from Jhansi towards Orchha. Their land was neither sufficient nor fertile enough to enhance productivity. As a result, sustaining the family financially became an arduous task. Over and above this, the Bundelkhand region is known for its prevailing water shortage. The immediate future seemed to offer little hope to them.

Both Arjun and his brother drifted away from home. His brother, presently settled in Gwalior, works in the construction sector and handles stone and tiling jobs. '*Woh hath se kaam karta hai* (He works with his hands),' Arjun told me, implying that his brother is a mason and not a civil contractor like him. In the mid-1990s, Arjun had left his village, initially for Rajasthan where he spent a few years working in a power plant construction project. He was involved in the site-work for few companies before landing up in Gurgaon. In between, he also shifted to a site in Shivpuri in Madhya Pradesh for a couple of years. Before he started contracting for small-time construction work, he had worked as a foreman in a private construction company. That had been his last full-time job. Arjun's wife is a homemaker. Their two sons are studying, one in a B.Com course and the other in an engineering college in Bhondsi in Haryana, about 15 km from his house. Like many others of his age, Arjun dreams of his children being employed in the service sector.

One may not find anything exceptional in Arjun's story and therein lies its relevance—the quintessential migrant, shifting his base time and again, in search of work. This is an example of 'horizontal social mobility', caused by the switching of livelihood from traditional agriculture in the village to the construction sector in the city. The changeover is occupational, spatial and socio-cultural, simultaneously. Arjun gradually acquired skill sets and knowledge through apprenticeship in real-life projects, became a small-time entrepreneur and gained 'vertical social mobility' by improving his socio-economic status in a new urban milieu very different from the one he originally belonged to. Eventually, the next generation will become educated and step into the service sector. Such transitions, from farmer to 'blue collar' work to 'white collar' job, can be found in vast numbers in Indian cities. These are anecdotes about the tenacity of common Indians, not always leading to the rags-to-riches stories that usually get reported.

Arjun and his family lived in a rented house at Chakkarpur. It is an erstwhile village, tucked discreetly into the glittering new development that surrounds it. They have changed a couple of houses, yet managed to stay within this locality since their arrival at Gurgaon. The present house is built on a plot of about 2,500 sq. ft. The front half of the plot, where the landlord has his residence, is approached from the main lane. A small gate opens directly onto the lane in front. The major part of the street frontage is occupied by a transport business run by the landlord's son.

'What does the landlord do?' I asked Arjun.

'*Saab, unko kuchh kaam karne ka zaroorat hi nahi hai. Makaan se hi unka bohut income hai* (Sir, he does not need to do any work. The rent collected from his house is more than enough),' Arjun replied.

A two-storey block at the back of the plot, accessible from the side lane is where the tenants stay. Each floor has a corridor at the centre with ten rooms lined up on either side. Arjun, his wife and two college-going sons share two rooms facing each other on both sides of the central corridor. Presently, they pay ₹10,000 as rent per month for two rooms. The two-storey block has 20 such 'houses' and the landlord earns about ₹1 lakh from it, without doing any other work. Chakkarpur is full of such houses that provide rental accommodation.

These transformed building blocks, by and large, are four storeyed. Arjun's landlord has another plot that he plans to build on soon, for similar rental accommodation. Such makeovers have already contributed to the increase in population, as well as to the change in community and the built environment. The population density of the place is also soaring accordingly.

'*Zyadatar Nepali log rehte hai. Woh log restaurant me kam karte hai. Log aate jaate rehte hai* (Most of them are Nepali and they usually work in restaurants. Tenants here keep on changing),' he said when asked about his neighbours. It was a reference to people from the north-eastern part of our country, albeit with a misinterpretation of their identity. In fact, a sizeable population from the Northeast resides in villages like Sikandarpur, Chakkarpur, Sukhrali and others, which has very recently prompted the Gurgaon police to depute officers from that part of the country. However, such a mix of different ethnic groups is a major departure from the caste-based community that traditionally stayed in Gurgaon's villages.

Chakkarpur, where around four thousand families stay, is within five minutes walking distance from the MG Road metro station. Nowadays in Delhi NCR, places around the metro corridor are colloquially referred to with respect to the distance from the metro station, underlining, to an extent, the success of the metro in Delhi so far.

In the context of Gurgaon, the metro has become a transport for the masses, especially for daily commuters to and from the city. Even at the beginning of the millennium, I saw a wide range of vehicles that used to transport people from Delhi to Gurgaon. The Qualis, once referred to by a friend as 'the modern-day bullock cart', used to be the most popular vehicle on this route, and was often seen overcrowded with passengers somehow managing to squeeze their heads inside. It was sad to witness people traveling in a herd for want of respectable and affordable transport options. Indeed, a certain degree of decency has returned with the arrival of the metro.

Along with the nearby villages of Nathupur and Sikandarpur, as well as many others strewn across the urban landscape of Gurgaon, Chakkarpur is a recurrent reminder of the Millennium City's rustic past, trapped within the shine and gloss of its present. However, there has been a continuous makeover of all these villages. People have changed, the built environment has thoroughly been modified and new activities have found their place in this altered urbanity. If out of curiosity, anyone looks for Chakkarpur on Google, it would appear to be a place full of health clubs, gyms, beauty parlours, doctor's clinics and similar facilities. Contemporary aspirations are on the rise.

While travelling by MG Road now, it is not easy to locate the street leading to Chakkarpur, almost hidden

Contradiction

behind Sahara Mall and its adjacent buildings. The other two accesses to the village are from the Galleria market to the south and Golf Course Road to the east. A nullah (drain) and a bundh to the east of the village separate it from DLF Phase IV, an upmarket residential neighbourhood.

Constructed during the British era, the present day nullah used to be an irrigation canal that supplied water to the agricultural fields nearby. The canal was protected by the bundh, a check dam at that time. Both the nullah and the bundh run for over 5 km from Chakkarpur in the north to Sector 56 in the south of the city. Over the years, the irrigation canal has been reduced to a filthy drain full of sewer and solid waste, while the bundh has become a derelict place for open defecation and a pasture for pigs. A few stretches allow limited movement of people from neighbouring squatter settlements and villages. This used to be the dirty underbelly of Gurgaon until recently, when the forest department of the state government and a city-based NGO took the initiative to rejuvenate the bundh and our architecture firm was roped in to design the project.

∽

DLF first acquired its land in Chakkarpur towards the end of 1980. Older villagers say that the price of land at that time was around ₹4-5 lakh per acre, which, of late, has shot up to anywhere over a lakh of rupees per square yard (1 acre = 4,840 square yards)—a whopping 1,200 times! Traditionally, village plots had the residence of the owner in front, with the byre for cattle at the back. Gradually, such open areas have been sacrificed, as we have seen with Arjun's landlord. Barrack-type buildings have been constructed to house migrants, almost like in the nineteenth century industrial cities. A plot where, at the most, two families stayed with about eight to ten members, now has 40 and more inhabitants.

Interestingly, the Chakkarpur precinct has been a favoured destination for the service class since the advent of Maruti. In 1986, Maruti Vihar, a housing complex with over 250 flats for the company staff, was built. Many owners, too, have let out their flats to young families. The legacy of company housing is reminiscent of labour welfare practice, before the open economy era that triggered the new making of Gurgaon. Later, when Maruti, among other companies, started hiring contractual labour, such gestures, meant to look after the labourers, were shelved. Almost three decades later in 2012, Maruti Suzuki India Ltd., having faced violent workers' protests at its Manesar plant near Gurgaon, reportedly coordinated with the government of Haryana for about 50 acres of land to build about 1,500 affordable flats for its workers in an attempt to improve their living condition.[56]

With newer constructions and increasing number of floors, the built fabric of the village has undergone complete transformation. Infrastructure, one of the weakest points of Gurgaon, is exposed to tremendous pressure due to such a drastic increase in the density of people. New socio-economic and ethnic groups have moved into several villages

Contradiction

where a considerable chunk of the original villagers moved out. These phenomena are symptomatic of many villages in Gurgaon that have been directly exposed to urbanization. The capricious contradiction of rapid economic growth reverberates in the urban life here.

Manuel Castells, a Spanish sociologist and US-based top academician associated with research on information society, communication and globalization, made certain profound observations regarding the socio-economic polarization in contemporary cities:

> [The dichotomy in cities] represents an urban structure that exists on the basis of interaction between opposite and equally dynamic poles of the new informational economy, whose developmental logic polarizes society, segments social groups, isolates cultures, and segregates the uses of a shared space.[57]

Traces of inherent existential conflicts within villages surface off and on. To 'promote inter-caste unity' in Gurgaon, a kabaddi tournament was organized at the government senior secondary school in Chakkarpur on Independence Day in 2016.[58] Over 30 teams representing different castes—Dalits, Yadavs, Jats, Gurjars, Banias, and others—from various villages across the NCR, participated in the event. The problem started when a Dalit team began winning over a team of Yadavs from Sikandarpur. The Yadav community, historically dominant in Chakkarpur village, allegedly made unsavoury remarks about the Dalits, threatened and assaulted them.

Over ten people were wounded in the resulting violence, with a couple of them hospitalized with head injuries and arm fractures. The local councillor reportedly denied any caste-based reason behind such an incident and blamed it on youngsters getting overexcited about the game. Nevertheless, when reports of caste-based abuses triggered the incident, it became difficult to ignore the stratified and somewhat gentrified society existing within the villages.

Gentrification is a process of rejuvenating any urban area by accommodating a middle-class population and, in turn, 'improving' the social and economic fabric of the place. This process is often seen when a new population starts replacing the older one in a place. Gurgaon's villages have been subjected to such a process of gentrification, with new sets of people coming in from all over the country. The dominance of traditional ethnic groups gradually melted away to some extent, making space for multi-ethnicity and diversity. However, such transitions have not always been smooth.

A spate of criminal attacks on people from the Northeast were reported in 2014–15 and later as well, revealing the vulnerability of certain ethnic groups in Gurgaon. The majority of them stay in villages like Nathupur, Sikandarpur and Chakkarpur and work in places like food joints, restaurants and call centres, which have extended working hours. Coincidentally, a number of such criminal incidents happened near villages, although it may not be apposite to draw an axiomatic correlation between the criminal activities and the villages.

Contradiction

In fact, these were the very villages that provided accommodation to the migrants. Over time, the changing social fabric might have experienced conflict issues that went beyond caste. Haryana Police has recently requested the deputation of mid-level personnel of northeastern origin as nodal officers. These ethnic groups, in turn, would feel more comfortable approaching this set of police personnel who might overcome the language barrier. This initiative is a response to the vulnerability of such groups in north India. In fact, Delhi Police, too, earlier recruited constables and set up separate units to handle crime against people from the Northeast.

Similarly, traditional villages have uncomfortable relationships with the new areas of Gurgaon. The intrinsic divide is social and/or economic. The rich or middle-income enclaves in Gurgaon are exclusive and protected from their immediacy. Irrespective of the context next door—enclaves developed by other developers, a village, a HUDA colony, an apartment block or anything else—an enclave is always guarded from all sides. 'Gurgaon is an example of how the government gives a hoot to its citizens,' a resident once said. The city demonstrates how a 'weakness' created due to the absence of support from the government in providing certain basic services, can be turned into a 'strength' to sell the idea of exclusive comfort.

Such exclusivity has led developers and residents to form their own private conclaves, with their own electricity, water, security, gym, swimming pool, club and all possible facilities.

In other words, each of these enclaves has its own world within its boundary. Beyond that circumscribed domain, schools and other special social circles exist, where children visit and meet each other. Otherwise, most of their time is spent within the limits of their own territory.

An enclave and its people meet directly with the city where they find people from their neighbouring places. Similar groups of neighbours may mingle, but diverse groups do not mix at all. The so-called mixing points or joints are malls, pubs, clubs, food joints and roads at large. An inherent psychological unease and social disquiet underlie these urban activity nodes. The other chosen option here is the Kingdom of Dreams-type of place—deliberately eclectic with high entry fees, yet interesting nonetheless.

Gurgaon is apparently a city of black and white with grey spaces missing. By grey, I do not mean dark or bad spaces, but spaces where black and white meet in multiple ways to create interesting mosaics. In other words, the city has exclusive and protected spaces within enclaves and the no-man's-land outside the enclaves. It lacks different types of public places where these two worlds mix to form in-between spaces. The differences in the physical appearances of buildings between these two types of places are very much visible. The economic stratification of urban society is, therefore, obvious and imminent where spatial proximity of realities is often in-your-face, and hence, uncomfortable. The social divide, however, exists beneath the surface.

Villages like Chakkarpur, Nathupur, Wazirabad and

Contradiction

others have plenty of rich people, agricultural landowners who decided to stay on their ancestral property. However, their way of living has changed in many ways. New luxury sedans and SUVs, BMWs and Audis are often seen parked in front of their houses, while one may find cattle in the backyard. Houses have been thoroughly refurbished with contemporary gadgets and high-end finishes. At the same time, one may also notice cow-dung cakes adorning several village walls, with their broken plaster and brick masonry. So, it is not unusual to find an odd heap of cow dung dumped on the road on which a swanky Audi or a Toyota Fortuner would pass by, carefully dodging the muck on the path. About two decades back, a scooter or a television set indicated the financial comfort of the owner. Now, the situation is completely different.

Bright sunlight beats down on the village street and bleaches the façades enclosing it, with sharp angles of shadows creating varied patterns on the ground. A retreating autorickshaw fills the frame and the apartment blocks of new Gurgaon loom over the skyline. Along the winding narrow street, wide junctions, or nodes, house spaces called chowks, a type of public square. A group of old men may be seen idling on a charpai (a traditional cot made of wood and cotton ropes), smoking their hookah, playing cards or gossiping. However, one must not miss the smartphones that they carry.

Farmers who sold their land at later dates made more money. By then, Gurgaon was well-established and urbanization was at its peak. Wazirabad village near Sector

55–56 is one of those places. All these villages carry visible traces of money, yet that would not guarantee them entry to the elitist niches of Gurgaon. The ensuing anxiety simmers in more than one way in the city's social spaces. Off and on, skirmishes surface.

In mid-2011, a group of village youth was reportedly refused entry into one of the pubs in Sahara Mall, resulting in a brawl. In response, villagers from Chakkarpur protested on MG Road and blocked entry to the Mall, demanding the arrest of the persons involved, as well as the closure of six pubs inside the mall. Indeed, this has not been a singular incident, many more have preceded and followed. Quite often, Sahara Mall happened to be the point of such conflicts.

In 2001, I conducted the first of many urban design studios with senior architecture students. The stretch of MG Road from Sikanderpur to IFFCO Chowk was chosen for a documentation, research and design proposal. Students came up with interesting urban design options. The making of public places was the central concern for them, which is quite different from what we see on the ground today.

The First India Place, JMD Tower, Metropolitan Mall and Beverly Park Housing blocks on either side of the road are prominent buildings on that stretch. Next to Sushant Lok, a large triangular chunk of land beside MG Road used to be vacant. Eventually, a couple of large buildings including MGF Metropolis and City Centre Mall have come up on that piece of land. The Bristol Hotel has been a witness to

Contradiction

transformations around it. The space where the triangular block of Emaar MGF building stands now, had some low-rise buildings and sheds owned by locals. From the Bristol till First India Place, there were no significant buildings on that side of the road. There were shacks, informal shops and vendors selling 'ganne ka ras' (sugar cane juice). Sahara Mall had not yet been built. The edges of the road were muddy and full of dust. MG Road was waiting for construction spectacles to happen.

Sahara Mall was built later, on a linear site, straddling the two worlds of Gurgaon—rustic ethnicity on one side and cosmopolitan urbanity on the other. This locational confluence has not been at ease ever since the project's realization. Such an uncomfortable coexistence of overtly differential societies has been a typical juxtaposition visible in many parts of the city.

The way in which the people of these two contrasting worlds react to each other's presence has been indicated in different observations. At times, the delicate balance of being is unsettled only to expose the schism. Stories of brawls and fights are often tagged with villagers reportedly flashing firearms. There is no doubt that similar instances have, indeed, occurred, but villages are painted as the sole source of law and order issues on the basis of hearsay. Many cosmopolitan residents might not have seen or experienced any such problem, yet they tend to avoid interacting with village people or going to places they fear are frequented by locals.

Security is also a big issue; either one secures oneself and one's family or one feels that nobody cares about them. Here people prefer to live a self-centred life, which stands out as a common thread of an otherwise disparate urban existence. One has to survive on one's own and hence, is forced to create notional, physical and social territories, each having its different limits, which often may or may not coincide. It almost sounds like a forest where inhabitants form herds and move around within certain unmarked, yet evident zones.

Insecurity is perceptual. For want of egalitarian public places, the confined spaces of malls, clubs, restaurants and pubs have become hang-out zones, expensive to visit and use. However, the youth of the villages who have seen money since their childhood, sometimes may not have easy access to these spots. The conflicts happen then.

People are open to business with moneyed villagers, but have prejudices about exchanging social spaces with them or their community. 'They are a bit feudal; they are patriarchal and culturally different from us... But we, the urbanites, have made the situation worse by blocking them out,' one of the residents of a gated society was quoted in an interesting story with anecdotal evidence, covered in *Business Standard* a few years back, about prevailing divisions in society in Gurgaon.[59] Often, colony residents may not have faced any odd behaviour from villagers, but they appear to be apprehensive. In turn, 'a safe distance' is maintained.

Over the last two and a half decades, the city has become home to multinational organizations from all across the

Contradiction

globe. The social constitution has become more cosmopolitan because people have come in from all over the country, in contrast with what happened in the initial years. During those days, people only came from Delhi; Gurgaon was perceived to be Delhi's southern extension, the way Noida and Faridabad were in the other directions. Residents primarily belonged to the working class population, albeit with different profiles. They lived in Gurgaon and worked in Delhi to begin with and slowly started working in Gurgaon when the corporates moved in. Later, many wealthy businessmen who sold their places in Delhi moved into Gurgaon. This made up for one part of Gurgaon's society: educated, cosmopolitan and affluent citizens. To such sections of Gurgaon, the existing villagers pose a serious disquiet. 'We want to integrate with them, but they don't know how to do so with us,' said one environment activist on being asked about the presence or the absence of social interactions and related contradictions in the city. I wondered if the villagers would say something similar about the 'enclave-dwellers'.

Upwardly mobile service sector workers enjoy an accomplished life and engaging work-home relationship. They are well-travelled and exposed to touches of luxury. Within Gurgaon, they drive down the road from one island where they stay to another island to work, play or shop. That is the connection they have with the city at large. The villagers on the other side are in a flux—the older generation valued a relaxed lifestyle, whereas their occupational status changed with the selling of farmland. The idyllic and sparsely built environment languished over time. Thus arise the contradictions when two societies come in contact with each other: on one side, cosmopolitanism fostered by the city's global networks and remarkable prosperity, and on the other, taciturn nativism.

There are instances when villagers, especially the youth, showed off their wealth to acquire the social status that they had longed for. Yet money alone could not ensure an entry into elite clubs or schools. This evasive social acceptability often thwarted access because their profile was not considered up to the mark. The glitz of certain places like pubs, that they wanted to share with the residents of the cosmopolitan world, were also kept away from the village youth. The clash at Sahara Mall was one such occasion when this happened.

Gun-toting continues to be a visible sight in Gurgaon. A decade and half back, I remember seeing one burly man openly showing off his pistol butt, peeping out of the case wrapped around his ribs. He had parked his big vehicle right after the border in the direction of Gurgaon, causing hindrance to the traffic on MG Road and was almost strolling on the highway with an arrogance of power in his movement while rebuking someone over a mobile phone. A decade-old shootout at Gurgaon's Euro International Kids School by a village-based, rich property dealer's son has not yet been forgotten.[60] Police was quoted in newspaper reports saying that the real estate dealers started carrying guns because of large cash dealings. Parents are still apprehensive about their wards mixing with pupils from the village.

Contradiction

Some villagers have apparently shifted their residence to gated enclaves so that their new address can ensure the child's admission to a 'reputed' school. Having sold their property in urban villages and made substantial profits, a chunk of the next generation of farmland owners—the original villagers—bought property in DLF colonies and shifted out. Urban villages, in turn, became densified with newcomers to Gurgaon, and with unchecked building activities and lack of infrastructure, are being increasingly pushed towards slum-like conditions. Arjun's story of Chakkarpur points to a similar process.

Kavita is a Gurgaon-based landscape architect running a firm with her architect husband. She had a short teaching stint at an architecture school in Gurgaon. At that time, she had a Hyundai Santro car, a very good hatchback. One day she told me that her chauffeur had a Maruti Esteem car, which was considered to be a good sedan those days. He used to park his car at her house and drive hers. I had found it a fascinating little anecdotal depiction of occupational mobility in Gurgaon.

The young driver had received a lot of hard cash when his father had sold a relatively small piece of land and bought his Esteem with that. His family had other cars as well. He was not particularly trained in any specific skills besides driving and hence, took up the job with Kavita. For him, it was like passing time in a pleasant manner and earning a bit on the side. This exemplified that money alone could not ensure social status and represented a dilemma faced by a number of villagers. Some of them, armed with the fast cash made from land deals, turned towards real estate brokerage and made a lot of money. These *nouveau riche* sprouted within village communities and contributed to the trend of 'showing off' their wealth rather callously.

A sensible resident explained the apparent contradictions in Gurgaon. 'To begin with, the villagers never interacted with the corporate residents like us, and we were also not keen on giving them the space to mingle with us. This boycott makes them agitated.' This is the subtext of a candid confession, touching the root of the discordance. Such a conception of difference, background, socio-cultural status and education to list only a few, creates a gulf among diverse groups in society.

The impending challenge is to have spaces that can lighten the social baggage carried by each group. Accessible public places can offer opportunities to bring people together. The urbanist's classical streets with people, activities, vibrancy and natural surveillance disappeared long ago, especially when automobiles and their excessive use in cities like Gurgaon and Delhi completely altered the scale and character of streets, converting them to high-speed transportation corridors. Urban public parks are few and far between in Gurgaon. Most of the green spaces are inside enclaves with highly restricted entry. Above all, when community green spaces are clubbed together to create a golf course in the city, the fascination for limited access open spaces for selective classes becomes evident yet again.

Contradiction

The tale of K.P. Singh of DLF extensively talks about the ways in which he interacted with villagers and became a part of their daily lives. When one is nice to villagers, they reciprocate, despite having different backgrounds and behavioural patterns. Some of them even extend an invite to their children's wedding or to a similar special family event. This is a clue about the manner in which interactions can level social incongruence. Now the question is, what is the suitable time and space that can offer opportunities for social interactions among diverse groups?

Housing delivery for the Economically Weaker Section (EWS) has its own problem in Gurgaon. In Delhi, the government was able to deliver a bit of lower-end housing, whereas in Gurgaon, that is totally absent. As per the Group Housing Scheme 1998, the income of members belonging to the EWS cooperative group housing societies should not exceed ₹2,500 per month. But in reality, in many of these societies, several members bought their shares from the original members by paying hefty sums to the extent of ₹25 lakh.

As per recent rules, a licenced colony must reserve 20 per cent of its plots (50–125 sq. m in size) in a residential plotted colony or 15 per cent of the total number of residential flats (of around 18.5 sq. m in size) in a group housing colony, for allotment to the EWS or Lower Income Group (LIG) category. Also, there is a mandatory lock-in period for selling these properties, to ensure that the original allottees stay. Despite all these conditions, there are complaints that hardly any eligible person from the EWS receives the land or flat earmarked for them in the licenced colonies.

Usually, these flats cost in the range of ₹15-30 lakh. A friend wanted to help their driver buy a flat for ₹18 lakh, but on the pretext of a certain court case, EWS people in that particular colony did not let the driver and his family settle there. The high market price of these flats or plots routinely encourages the selling of the property to more affluent people in the colony, and in turn, they are used as stores, small offices or for other ancillary purposes. It is observed that people living in the flats or houses allotted to the EWS often have gadgets, equipment and luxury cars.

The colony layout itself is not inclusive and many a time, EWS and LIG areas in the same colony are accessed separately, as if they belong to different poles. In some of the high-end housing enclaves, the domestic help use separate lifts. A palpable social separation is an inseparable layer to the way of life in Gurgaon. The lower economic strata and the indigenous villagers are not welcome in the cocooned spheres of the conclaves and high-end public realms of malls, shopping places and golf clubs. The rich in Gurgaon stay in their exclusive realms of existence. A very different form of 'untouchability' prevails in the city. It is unfair on the one hand to single out wealthy citizens for all the evils in the society, and on the other, to hold them responsible

Contradiction

for providing proper accommodation to the lower strata of society. Here, the government's role comes into play, to ensure respectable living conditions for all sections of society, which is unfortunately absent in Gurgaon.

As one may have gathered by now, Gurgaon, since its inception, has been an example of a city where the state has shrugged off its responsibility in all possible ways. It is a city of the private, by the private and for the private, to appropriate an overused phrase. Here, land, capital and the city-making process have been vested in the hands of the private, thereby baring the stark social inequities. The state could have displayed much-needed alacrity to intervene when required, but that is not the case. Landed elites and real estate developers forged an arrangement to bypass the state and managed to keep the poor out of the conception of Gurgaon's urbanity. Over the years, the state has been oblivious to this issue and is continuing with its blissful ignorance, letting stories of differences surface, instead of inculcating a sense of cohesion.

Gurgaon needs public places very badly, where every section of society can gather without any inhibition and hindrance. The government, so far, has not understood it. In turn, the responsibility has been left to private developers who have not delivered and have let the culture of consumption swamp the spirit of public spaces in the city. This is a classic example of 'passing the buck'. Metaphorically speaking, no one has really cared about it thus far, as most of them were too occupied in arranging their domestic plenitude.

In recent times, a new culture of forging 'partnerships' between private corporations and citizens is emerging. Many issues are 'imagined' to be addressed and corrected through the interventions of citizens and their groups. The underlying feeling is that a lot of 'bad' has happened already and somehow the city needs to be improved. The social responsibility of private citizens and corporates is being tapped into and private capital is being sourced to 'solve' urban problems in Gurgaon. This approach, at times, has shown good results, and should be encouraged. However, considering the yawning gaps that need to be filled, such attempts can only supplement the planning and implementation initiatives that should be taken up by large developers and the government.

A wider perspective would reveal that contradictions in Gurgaon are not only social, but also environmental. Urbanization, in general, encroaches upon natural assets. Especially when this process is ad hoc, piecemeal and opportunistic, with the sole motive of earning money, natural assets are the first things to be sacrificed. Gurgaon is a case in point and, in that sense, symptomatic of urban growth in India. Certain aspects of urbanization here became trendsetters, but the way irresponsible intervention has been made in the natural layers, Gurgaon is typical of any other unknown town in the country.

Contradiction

By the end of 2000, I started visiting Gurgaon regularly for work that continued for the next 12 years. I travelled by MG Road. Soon after entering the city, one approached DLF Corporate Park, an office complex, and Garden Estate, a high-end housing colony, both on the right side. The road would then lead straight into Sikanderpur village, bifurcating it into two. There was no bypassing the village. That particular stretch of the road was narrow and lined with shops selling building material. Gurgaon was an upcoming and potentially thriving construction site. Just before Sikanderpur, there was a narrow culvert with a nullah flowing under it, the site of a traffic bottleneck every day. Initially, the culvert over the nullah was widened to open up the constricted vehicular flow. But, one fine day, the nullah was converted into a piped drain, buried underground and a new road, popularly known as the Sikanderpur Bypass, came up.

This is the story in most of the cities where age-old water channels are either converted into roads, forced to become dirty drains or obstructed at some point or the other. As a result, most of the cities in India have not recognized the potential of such natural elements. Such an insensible attitude has turned these spaces into urban backyards. With no clear agenda or vision for these waterways, many cities have witnessed the sprouting of squatter settlements along its canal edges, with no provision for basic services, whether it is Tolly's Nullah in Kolkata or Buckingham Canal in Chennai or Mullassery Canal in Kochi. The adjoining water channels have become open toilets.

Most of these networks are converted into piped drains, thereby nullifying the possibility of the water seeping into the underground water layer and recharging the groundwater. The storm water from the catchment area can only drain into the nullah at limited points since it has been covered from the top. Due to these irresponsible constructions, urban flooding is experienced in every city.

Historically, the Sikanderpur nullah used to be one of the many rainwater streams, coming down the slope of the Aravallis and irrigating a little bit of agricultural land that Gurgaon had once upon a time. Traces of that stream can still be found in the form of a large-sized longish water body and a dry winding stretch behind the present-day Global Business Park adjacent to Dronacharya metro station. Recently, I have heard that a couple of NGOs teamed up with some benevolent and responsible citizens with the aim of rejuvenating this water body.

Interestingly, one may find a relationship between these storm water canals, earlier the source of water and irrigation, and the adjacent erstwhile villages. In Delhi, too, the majority of the 'urban villages' are next to water channels which, over time, have been turned into drains. There have been quite a few failed initiatives to rejuvenate the drains of Delhi. Two types of urban responses have surfaced among Delhi experiments: one that covered the nullah to make public spaces and another that created a flyover or road on it. Interestingly, both these approaches are being followed elsewhere, uncritically.

Contradiction

A couple of decades back, a storm water channel used to flow from the ridge through Sector 56 in Gurgaon; it has now run dry. Over the years, the boundary walls of various types of complexes were built on its edges, always trying to grab an extra bit of land from it. At some point, the flow of the nullah was obstructed in one way or the other. Yet, when seen from the top, its traces are visible as a meandering green line in the city map. Unfortunately, vanishing blue lines have been a scandalous character of the twenty-first-century cities, with the spectre of urban floods looming large. Gurgaon is no exception to it, as time and again, it comes to a halt after a heavy monsoon.

The ridge to the east of Gurgaon is a part of the Aravallis, the oldest mountain range in India and a fold mountain created when the collision between landmasses resulted in folding up of the land, literally. The ridge and the canals, the storm water system for replenishing the land, had a symbiotic relationship. These channels used to flow from east to west through the settlements of Gurgaon. Before the villages of Chakkarpur near MG Road or Wazirabad located near sector 56, some of these channels meet another nullah running parallel to the ridge and today's Golf Course Road, the neo-glamorous address in the town.

This nullah is over 5-km long, running north-south of Gurgaon. At some point in time, it used to meet a tributary of the Najafgarh drain, once a rivulet and now a highly dirty drain flowing through the capital of the country. The water course is edged by an earthen bundh, a check dam protecting nearby settlements like Wazirabad and Chakkarpur, from any possible flood. It gives an indication of the volume of water that used to flow through this channel, which also doubled as the irrigation canal for the adjoining cultivated land. The continuity of the bundh is ruptured by three main east-west roads connecting Golf Course Road.

The bundh, shaded by a lot of invasive vilayati kikar trees, is under the jurisdiction of the Department of Forest of the government of Haryana, whereas the nullah flowing next to it is under the HUDA. The nullah was full of plastic and all possible garbage. The bundh was used as a dumping ground and for open defecation. This long stretch of forest land, in the middle of high-end residential housing enclaves, schools and hospitals, was abused and left in a sad state. This was Gurgaon's urban backyard used out of desperation by marginalized people, by domestic helps for walking or cycling on a rough uneven land to reach their workplaces and by pigs and other animals.

The revival of such abandoned spaces can energize the urban landscape by creating a healthy environment for outdoor leisure and an alternative movement corridor for city-dwellers. A Gurgaon-based NGO, iamgurgaon, in collaboration with leading corporate houses from the city and the Forest Department of the state government, took up a long-drawn ambitious initiative to rejuvenate the bundh. The NGO involved our architecture and landscape firm, VSPB Associates, as consultants to draw up a design proposal. Vina Verghese Biswas, the landscape architect of

Contradiction

the project said, 'On my first visit to the project site in September 2015, I found that it was absolutely inaccessible. Garbage was strewn everywhere. There was a repulsive stench. We had to dodge between thorny scrubs. The challenge to transform it into a green mobility corridor was manifold!'

A public place was envisioned with a universally accessible linear park, tucked away from the noise and dust of busy roads, combined with an alternate mobility corridor providing non-motorized linkages with walking and cycling tracks for all and sundry. The whole 5.2-km length of the bundh has already been rejuvenated to create a public park planted with indigenous species and it is being used by morning-walkers and joggers, and for short distance travel by foot or by cycle from one part of the city to another. A lot of domestic help, the majority among them being women, use this space for their movement with ease and comfort. This forest corridor has formed a 'green lung' for Gurgaon and a natural setting for leisure facilities for the adjoining residential areas. Tree plantation by corporate houses and cultural activities by children from city schools are some of the social interaction events that have already taken place in this park. The award-winning collaborative project has converted this otherwise forgotten space into a popular hotspot set in a natural setting.[61]

On one of my site visits to this park, I met a lady who was cycling to her place of work. She had migrated from north West Bengal and stayed in a slum near Wazirabad village. She worked as a domestic help in a few houses adjacent to this bundh corridor. She was extremely pleased to have a clean and 'nice' place for her transit. Earlier, it was highly inconvenient to cycle on the uneven mud surface of the bundh with dirt strewn all around. It was also scary to traverse, with groups of men sitting and drinking local liquor in places.

When solar-powered street lights were fixed in the park, more residents and especially ladies started using the corridor more comfortably. I have often encountered villagers who wait in the park after accompanying a relative admitted in Paras Hospital, which shares its boundary with the bundh-turned-park. Such a project points out how cooperation and coexistence between diverse stakeholders in the city can come together to contribute to a better environment and society shared by all across the spectrum.

'The bundh is going to change the city. I have seen that everybody living close by is happy to see it being done,' one of the visitors told me. She came to participate in a planting drive on the bundh, undertaken by one of Gurgaon's IT companies. The energy and the feel-good spirit in those young people were easy to sense. It was a cloudy day and we were standing on the stretch of the bundh that shares its boundary with Paras Hospital. What she said was right, I thought; the hospital also got such a good place next to it, without really doing much to improve its surroundings. The patients and everyone else using the adjacent rooms will be able to look at a clean and well-designed place. People, at large, can reap the benefits. Dirty plastic dumped in heaps over the last 20 years was cleaned from the nullah, allowing it to flow better.

'People used to throw their garbage there,' the site supervisor pointed to an area, 'and a few days back, when someone was cleaning that place, one guy started shouting at him to stop. Then, a lady came out of a house and started shouting back, supporting the cleaning act.' Once an area is cleaned, people usually do not mess up that space. I also met a priest whose temple was about 500 m from where the hospital abuts the bundh. A water body next to it has almost dried up. The priest said that they tried to save it, but could not, and he was extremely happy to see the rejuvenated pond. Everybody started owning the place. That is how urban public places get their 'natural proprietors', an idea that Jane Jacobs, the great Canadian-American urban theorist and activist, propagated in the 1960s while criticizing modern urban planning vehemently.

The bundh and nullah are the neglected components of the historical irrigation system that harnessed storm water down the slope of the ridge of the Aravallis. The ridge itself has not been spared of ceaseless encroachment, with people always trying to grab more. The roads on the ridge have undoubtedly helped connectivity, but they have also opened up the possibility of threatening the forest and overall biodiversity of the ridge. Perhaps the last surviving real forest patch of the ridge in the whole of NCR, the Mangar Bani forest, spread over about 500 acres of land on the Gurgaon-Faridabad road, also encountered serious threats when developers tried to usurp the area showing utter disrespect to its rich ecology and history.[62]

Situated in the south Haryana region of the Aravallis, this forest area, about 20 km away from Gurgaon, is at the boundary of Faridabad and Gurgaon districts, adjoining Delhi. Connectivity to this place has been enhanced considerably by the widening of the highway. Serious concerns had been raised since the beginning of the millennium about the far-reaching implications of real estate development, yet the land-grabbing continued unabated. Finally in June 2016, the forest and the 500-m. buffer zone in Gurgaon and Faridabad districts were demarcated and notified as a 'no-construction zone' by the Haryana government.

Mangar Bani is historically a unique community-conserved forest and not a state-protected one, signifying the sensibility among traditional communities about concerns for sustainability, a clichéd expression superficially cultivated in urbane society. Like many other 'ecosystem' people who live in a place for generations, understand and contribute to its ecology, the Gurjars of Mangar, too, have a deep respect inculcated in their social and cultural lives for the flora and fauna around. In popular perception, the Gurjars are tagged as rude for their not-so-sophisticated behaviour and many of the conflicts in and around Gurgaon are sometimes credited to these groups. Contrary to such generic observations, the community's sentience about the forest is remarkably wholesome in comparison to the gated communities taking

Contradiction

part in the unsustainable energy-consuming activities in almost every corner of the city.

The belief that the Mangar Bani forest was the abode of the beloved saint Gudariya Das Baba informs its sanctity. The community's respect for the forest originated from their devotion to the beloved saint, who advised them not to cut the Dhau trees of the forest.[63] This is a story of the knowledge and belief system constructed by intertwining myth with nature, which was handed down across generations. Thus, a nature-culture symbiotic relationship was produced by upholding the 'genius loci' of a place. Such practices and cultural constructs are quite common for the people who live close to nature. I have observed traces of similar nature-culture relationships in the Sundarbans, in a completely different ecological setting far away from Mangar Bani. But there too, people live close to nature.

The whole issue once again revolves around the ambiguity of land ownership. Mangar Bani, being non-fertile land in the Aravallis, was 'common land' over which the village panchayat had control. In the 1970s, an administrative order brought about a change in ownership, from panchayat to the community, and landowning villagers in the community got their share of the common land and the Mangar Bani.[64] The landless villagers were left out: once again, land policy excluded the marginalized, a practice that is common even in the making of urban Gurgaon. On paper, a villager owning 2 per cent of agricultural land in the village would own the same percent of common land. In the next move, villagers were allowed to sell their share of common land. The final blow of privatization was to allow new shareholders, portioning the old common land purchased from the villagers. Once mining stopped and the Gurgaon-Faridabad Road was augmented to increase accessibility, the real estate activities in this area began to surface.

Socio-environmental activists and media campaigned together to somehow frustrate the efforts of overenthusiastic developers and outsiders. On social media, campaigns to protect the forest were started by groups of students, environmentalists, filmmakers, activists and responsible citizens.

Although Mangar Bani is not located in urban Gurgaon, it epitomizes the inclusion of natural resources in traditional community-based practices, in comparison to the individualistic attitude of urbanization. In place of traditional communities, new citizen-groups are formed in cities, of people who are working in their own little ways to promote sustainability. In Gurgaon too, such groups are prevalent.

༄

Many a time, I have driven through Sultanpur to avoid the peak hour rush on MG Road and entered Sector 56 via Faridabad-Gurgaon Road, where the present-day Golf Course Extension Road starts. Near Ghata village, at one point, boundary walls demarcating plots could be seen, with

Contradiction

a developer's signboard announcing ridge-view colonies. The construction was eventually stopped and the Aravallis were somewhat unscathed for the time being. The forest on the ridge, however, was not well cared for. It was brown, barren in places and full of invasive species. A lot of construction debris was dumped on the highway beside the forest, with no concern for the natural resources of the ridge and the forest.

Like Mangar Bani, a sacred forest protected by a traditional community, citizen groups, corporates and the government department joined hands to try and salvage a certain quality of life of the forest. Thus, one part of the Aravallis in Gurgaon was reclaimed and turned into a biodiversity park. This park and the linear park on the restored bundh in Wazirabad are 'urban commons' that anyone can access without any inhibition. 'We grew up elsewhere, but our children were born and brought up here in Gurgaon. This is their city. We should build a better place for them at least,' a member of an active citizen-group told me. It is indeed about intergenerational equity: if we have had a quality childhood, we should also ensure a similar or better one for the next generation. Environmental activism is essentially hinged upon such a realization.

REFLECTION

On the City

> Gurgaon has a huge base of people who are moving forward, young, energetic and enterprising.... Gurgaon is only 20 years old. A city that has grown so fast within such a short span of time is bound to have its share of problems. Could it have been planned better? Yes. Should it have been planned better? Definitely. Whenever I have a visitor who has been to Gurgaon over the years, they look around and wonder that it is remarkable how the city is developing! I know that most people in Delhi wonder whether it is a complete marvel or a complete mess! Those of us who live there—we love it.

Pramod Bhasin, Genpact's former CEO, was delivering a passionate speech at the inauguration of the Aravalli Utsav at India Habitat Centre (IHC) in Delhi in 2017. It was a very pleasant early November evening. He was speaking at the amphitheatre towards the back of the central courtyard of IHC.

Reflection

The audience was attentive. A lot of them could not find any space to sit on the steps of the amphitheatre; some squeezed themselves up on planters to sit. The rest were standing. In the middle of complete darkness, the stage was brightly lit like an island. The sound reverberated against the brick walls of the building around. I could see a glimpse of the moon above our head, through the metal trellis spanning across the courtyard. IHC, designed by the master architect Joseph Allen Stein, is a wonderful example of an urban architecture successfully offering a meaningful space for public cultural activities. It was indeed a magical setting!

That evening, the majority of the audience was from Gurgaon. It was a different crowd from the one that usually flocks IHC—the quasi-ethnic, block-printed dresses were swept away by gauzy chiffons, and stylized cotton half-jackets and kurtas were replaced by dark-coloured suits. Audis and BMWs were parked all over the parking. Gurgaon, I thought, had taken over the intellectual space of Delhi, right in the heart of the city.

Aravalli Utsav was a combination of exhibitions, book release events, discussions and related activities. The exhibition was an innovative and experiential attempt to capture the materials, landscape, people, flora and fauna of the Aravallis. I was captivated by the vibrancy and the richness of the hill range that is like our next door neighbour. The stare of an owl, the kingfisher picking up a fish from a shallow waterbody, the natural artistry of the tree foliage and the texture of the rocks were some of the photo exhibits that will remain in my mind for a long time.

We often encounter the hills around different corners of Delhi NCR, but have not really explored those adequately. I wondered what made the residents of Gurgaon take the initiative to showcase the Aravallis that played a vital role in shaping the terrain in northwest India, spreading over about 700 km from Palanpur near Ahmedabad in Gujarat to Raisina Hill in central Delhi, through Rajasthan and Haryana. Was it the energy and youthfulness of the city that Pramod Bhasin mentioned in his speech? I am yet to find a clear answer, but Gurgaon's dynamism was visible in more ways than one.

The exhibition also included the biodiversity park spread over approximately 380 acres, which, like the linear park project at Wazirabad bundh, was a collaborative effort between government organizations, corporates and an active group of citizens. Immediately on entering Gurgaon via MG Road, one may see on the right, the gabion wall punctuated with a cement jaali—that is the boundary wall for the Aravalli Biodiversity Park. The land used to be a mining site and still bears some of those scars. The park is a city-level forest with native species of plants from the northern Aravalli, sheltering rich flora and fauna while also acting as an effective groundwater recharge zone. This large, green, open space, with features like nature trails, tracks for walking and cycling and an amphitheatre, has also become a popular space in the city for recreational activities. A performing arts programme called Gurgaon Utsav has also become a prominent event held at the amphitheatre.

Reflection

Such a project, some critics feel, may put a stop on the use of open spaces like urban commons, an area for the local community for grazing animals. About 30-40 acres of village land also falls within the present territory of the park. Earlier, this used to be like a peri-urban space beside Delhi. The village community used to live differently and they had sufficient livestock for agricultural purposes. The socio-economic conditions have changed over time. The urban commons may also be subject to modification in the present context, from a grazing field to an urban open space with multiple dimensions.

'So, we have planted 350 acres and if I look at it from other way round, that is one way of protecting the land for the government. A lot of nearby villagers visit and it has become a community space where people from all backgrounds interact,' says Latika Thukral, a regular visitor to the park and one of the key members of the NGO behind the park's revitalization. Since 2010, over 50 corporates and a similar number of schools, a large number of children and citizens have planted about a 100,000 saplings that brought about the park's new avatar.[65] This is a technique to ensure that a city-space is appropriated by the people at large. When users feel that they are a part of it in some way or the other, a place for the community comes into being.

To reiterate my point, when the state is incognizant of the needs of its cities and the concerns of citizens residing there, urban problems are perceived to be answered through private capital and citizen initiatives. Gurgaon epitomizes such a situation. Besides the erstwhile villagers, the corporate and business elites who came here in the late 1980s and 90s, had to run after their respective careers and, often simultaneously, concentrated on bringing up their children.

Career growth and immediate family attention left little time for other things. Most of them, by now, have reached a stable point in their professional lives. Their children have also grown up and joined colleges and universities, older children might have even joined the job market. Some of them may have moved out of the city, either to study or to work. Many Gurgaon citizens, as a result, have some mind space to carve out time and energy to look at the city around them and ponder what the place offers to their children, who may continue to live and work here. The answer, I can assume, is not very positive at present.

For a lot of things that the state government and the city authority were supposed to do, well-meaning people from the civic society came forward. They acted like pressure groups, trying to work in partnership with government organizations to plug loose ends.

Over the years, I have noticed that most commentators take an either-or position with respect to Gurgaon. They either like the place or abhor it. Once, I attended a book release held at the India International Centre in Delhi. The book was an edited collection on contemporary urbanism in India. By the time I reached, everyone had already entered the seminar hall and the discussion was about to start. Having managed to gobble a quiche and a cup of coffee, I

Reflection

entered the room. The audience was formidable, boasting known names from the literary and academic realms of the city.

The book included theoretical and case-based essays from writers across the country. The panellists were supposed to have read the book in advance, which perhaps, a few of them could not have undertaken! At least, it seemed to be so, from the contours of the conversations that unfolded thereafter. A couple of discussants somewhat formed their views on the positives and negatives of Gurgaon and limited the conversation to that, as if it was the only available example of urbanism in India. Again, the opinion was extremely polarized. One of them could only see the wrongs in the city, in terms of lack of basic services and public transport, unsustainability in architectural materials and how that brand of urbanization had destroyed natural aspects. The others described the city's high share in business, the opportunities it offered, and how economic migrants had improved their life there. It was an interesting debate, but it constantly digressed from the central content of the book released that day.

Many of the harshest critics of Gurgaon are not the ones who stay there. It does not mean that those who stay in Gurgaon do not criticize it. Many Gurgaon residents, too, are vehement critics of the city. However, a lot of these detractions somehow remind me of Chandigarh, designed by the master architect Le Corbusier. Residents of the city love it, but its planning, inspired by High Modernism, drew many criticisms as well, one of the best coming from James C. Scott, an anthropologist and political scientist from Yale University.[66] Possibilities of any meaningful comparison between Gurgaon and Chandigarh would be far-fetched. In fact, there is hardly any point of coincidence in the production and representation of these two cities, except that both ushered in the ambition of a new era, albeit in different times in history.

Few may misinterpret this particular discussion as a comparison between the incomparable, which it does not intend to be. Instead, it is a rather innocuous attempt to place a newer city in perspective with its celebrated predecessors. Delhi and Chandigarh were both conceived and shaped by comprehensive state-driven planning. Delhi was formed by a Master Plan document, whereas Chandigarh was planned by the master and his ideology, and none of those has been instrumental in modelling Gurgaon. Neither any master planner, nor any rigorous planning document catalyzed its formation. A value-loaded ideology was also missing in the process.

Both in Delhi and in Chandigarh, modern planning was applied, 'with the redistribution and reconfiguration of land by the state'.[67] Redistribution of land, in general and also as used in planning for the upper strata, would underscore possible foundations being laid out for economic prosperity in the future. And, for the lower strata of society, it was about equity, social respect, removal of caste-based spatial ghettos and the like. Redistributed land was meant for citizens of

Reflection

the country, irrespective of their caste, creed and religion.

Modern planning was often delivered from a lofty ideological pedestal. The intention was noble but utopian, and the delivery was far from satisfactory. Post-independence Delhi was an aspirational city for new citizens, breaking away from pre-existing social and spatial stratifications and providing economic opportunities in modern society. Chandigarh, Scott writes, was synonymous with 'the promotion of modern technology in a new capital that would dramatize the values that the new Indian elite wished to convey'.[68]

Gurgaon, more than any of its contemporary counterparts, has been a city to go to for the fulfilment of ambitions. The amalgamation of land and its redistribution took place, but the purpose was not to address social inequity; instead, it was intended to profit from the price of land and the property built on it. If land was an ideological edifice for Delhi, in Gurgaon it has been an empirical and quantitative entity. If the representation of new architecture and the city that Corbusier built in Chandigarh were in tune with the then mainstream 'international' trend, in Gurgaon, in the absence of a master architect, the architecture represented a desire to replicate and often reproduce stereotypes of the prevalent global practice.

I have been inquisitive to know what one likes about Gurgaon. 'I like it being a small city with everything nearby. We came at the right time, grew with the city and came to know everyone around. We formed our social circle.

Children had their school circle, too. We have had this small world of our own,' one of the residents told me. It is a very interesting point—the city's operating scale helps one overcome the usual anonymity of a big city.

According to the 2011 census, Gurgaon's urban population was less than 9 lakh; some of the cities with a similar population range at that time were Bareilly, Aligarh, Moradabad, Jalandhar and Bhubaneswar. If one looks at the literacy level of those cities as a simplistic indicator, Gurgaon and Jalandhar were at 86–87 per cent and the rest of the cities in that bracket were at less than 70 per cent except Bhubaneswar, which was hovering at over 90 per cent.

Another recent report from the beginning of 2017 suggested that the total wealth held in Gurgaon, Pune and Chennai was around $110 billion, $180 billion and $150 billion, respectively.[69] A quick conversion to Indian rupees gives us the massive figure of around 7 lakh crore for Gurgaon. The population of Pune was a little over 3 million, about three and a half times more than Gurgaon, and Chennai was marginally over 7 million, almost eight times Gurgaon's population.

A rudimentary calculation would indicate that Gurgaon, despite its smaller population, has more per capita wealth, notwithstanding the wide economic schism existing across different groups of people. With countless multinationals and Indian companies operating from here, it also offers job opportunities with both horizontal and vertical social and economic mobility. A relatively smaller size, combined with

Reflection

ample opportunities for earning, such as in a big city, is a combination unique to Gurgaon.

~

There is a long bucket list of essential requirements for a civilized city that have been missing in Gurgaon. Absence of a storm water drainage network, an inadequate sewage system, an inappropriate solid waste disposal system, including the disposal of construction waste, shortage of water and electricity, depletion of the water table, high energy consumption, urban flooding and lack of public transport are some of the prominent issues in Gurgaon.

'Gurgaon has no proper storm water drainage plan, which is our first problem and then comes the problem of sewage. Another problem is garbage disposal. In the present system, garbage is dumped in Bandhwari, but a lot of work is being done trying to segregate at the source,' a resident who is also an active participant of many citizen initiatives informed me. The Bandhwari plant, situated along Gurgaon-Faridabad Road, has been shut since June 2013 and the garbage from Gurgaon and Faridabad was being dumped there without any treatment.

Finally, an agreement was signed in mid-August 2017, among Haryana urban local bodies, municipal corporations of Gurgaon and Faridabad and a private party to develop Haryana's first integrated solid waste management project and to set up a waste-to-energy plant. The concessionaire will be also responsible for setting up a complaint redressal system for waste management and use e-rickshaws for waste collection. They will also showcase the entire collection and transportation of waste online for public preview to ensure transparency.[70]

Several gated enclaves tried to propagate and train people on how to segregate the waste at source; some colonies also made attempts to set up treatment within their compounds. In 2016, initiatives in the Magnolias to set up a waste management plant were reported and a similar plant had also been set up at the Garden Estate.[71] Many other upscale condominiums and residential colonies, too, have acted on solid waste management, and waste separation at the household level has begun.

Magnolias, with an area of more than 25 acres, is a high-end housing complex on Golf Course Road. Solid waste is segregated and processed at their plant and is turned into compost for horticultural use. Organic waste, amounting to about 350 kg a day, and the rest, the recyclable waste, are collected in two separate bins so that the former is converted into manure while the latter is further sorted for necessary recycling.[72] The remaining waste is sent to Bandhwari. The occupants and the domestic helps are also updated on the waste management system of the condominium. The compost can be collected free of cost by residents for use in gardening. The solid waste management system has been a part of the project from the beginning, alongside which the complex also has rainwater harvesting pits for groundwater

Reflection

recharge and a 400 kilolitre per day sewage treatment plant. The developer reportedly spent around ₹17 lakh to install the waste management system there.[73]

So far, it sounds excellent. The development seemed to be very responsive to the environment, so I decided to delve into a bit more.

I looked up the Magnolias' website, run by its developer. The flat sizes, the so-called 'super built-up area', range between 5,800 and 9,800 sq. ft. with five bedrooms, and the cost is between ₹14–25 crore with a whopping per square foot cost of about ₹25,000. The housing complex has a little less than 600 flats. To install the solid waste treatment plant, each owner's share would have been about ₹3,000, which is equivalent to about 1/8th of the price of only 1 square foot of each flat. The cost of all recyclable measures like treating of garbage and waste water as well as rainwater harvesting, will come to, at the most, 1/4th the price of only one square foot of each flat. For such wealthy owners, this seems a miniscule cost, but the cost-benefit ratio is high.

One of my architect friends in Gurgaon told me that, of late, two types of housing are being built: one is the Magnolias-type of high-end model and the other is packaged under the affordable housing slogan. Such 'super-expensive' housing projects, he felt, have very limited takers. Gurgaon is no longer as appealing as it used to be. 'In that price, people can buy a house in Delhi, and Delhi is *Delhi*, you see,' he said.

The list of features that housing projects boast nowadays includes environmental measures like waste treatment and rainwater harvesting. The concept of cost factor is replaced by the cost-benefit factor and, in the process, eco-friendly measures help to repackage the project with an extra topping of sustainability, to put it rather bluntly. For buyers, it is psychologically comforting that they intend to be sensible to their living environment without inflicting further damage on it and by leaving a better place for their successors. An ideology of intergenerational equity works in this way.

What happens to the cheaper housing? Will it be too expensive for those flats to include sustainability measures? If we consider a flat elsewhere, at 1/4th the per-square-foot price of the ones in Magnolias, the cost of recyclable measures in those cheaper flats will be half the price of one square foot. Lower the cost of the flat, higher the proportionate share of expenses for sustainable measures. This is the thumb rule and both developers and buyers shall have to agree on an optimum cost when affordability and environment are both addressed.

All these efforts at the level of plots and colonies are welcome steps that can reduce the amount of garbage handed over to the city, with the eventual goal of reducing the dependency on landfills and a centralized system. In turn, we may get a clean city. Everyone, by now, realizes that considering the way cities are expanding, it will become almost impossible to handle any type of waste at the city level and decentralization has to be adopted to keep cities clean. In Gurgaon, which many consider to be a set of enclaves, such systems of enclave-wise waste handling would be the way

Reflection

to a real solution. To encourage these efforts, the municipal corporation should provide adequate incentives. Though this attempt at self-sufficiency in solid waste handling makes a lot of sense, it also highlights the ineffectiveness of the state-run system.

༜

While driving down the Gurgaon-Faridabad Road, one often encounters heaps of construction debris by the roadside. 'Almost 35,000 cubic meters of construction and demolition waste were used to prepare the base of the paving in one kilometre length of the Wazirabad bundh project. We were able to clean and reuse that much waste for a public project,' Vina informs me.

Construction seems to be going on everywhere, be it Delhi or Gurgaon. However, Gurgaon does have some specificities. The construction cranes and JCBs frantically clearing up sites and dumping debris are the common sights here. 'You have to plan a city so that there is space for kids to walk around. This thought has not gone into the making of the city and a lot of it is the developers' fault. They only looked at the city as a money-making project,' a friend laments.

The Gurgaon-Faridabad Road, when seen on Google Earth, looks like a python snaking through the forest of the Aravallis. It has undoubtedly improved connectivity between these two cities. However, the present roadway has also destroyed the slope of the ridge by modifying the existing slope so that it can turn at will. The earlier two-lane road was a slow-moving one, trying to negotiate the slopes and the bends. At times, overloaded trekkers used to get stuck on a steep slope. At one point was just before the present connection to Golf Course Extension Road, the highway abruptly took a sharp bend to open up a wide view of the Aravalli landscape. In winter, the sight used to be mystical!

The Faridabad road was later connected by a wide bypass from MG Road, once again by chiselling off the ridge. Each time a new road was made, newer areas were opened up for development and, piece by piece, Gurgaon was built. Someone said sarcastically that this city can be called the 'united enclaves of Gurgaon'. To many, it is not a city as a whole. Delhi is also, to a great extent, divided into parts, but there is a sense of a whole in its Master Plan, albeit that notion of wholeness has long been left behind. Gurgaon is a completely different iteration in this regard. It never had an idea of a 'whole' city at all.

How does one read a city like this? To make out something about a place, a number of approaches have been discussed in various fields, including in sociology, geography, planning, urban design and others. Urban design is a disciplinary specialization of architecture that helps one understand, comment on, visualize and design a city and various parts of it. My discussion traverses along and across such conceptual contours and touches upon two key ways to observe a city like Gurgaon: collage and assortment.

Reflection

Over the years, urban theorists have given different accounts of the city, trying to address questions like what it is, how it is and what it should be. Fredric Jameson, an eminent literary critic and political theorist, talked about postmodernity and postmodern cities at great length.[74] He was disappointed with postmodernity's adoption of the historical past for mere stylizations, or 'pastiche'. Gurgaon is a case in point that underlines several of his influential critiques. We discussed those assumptions in earlier chapters while talking about the 'impression' of a city. Interestingly, Jameson commented rigorously around the beginning of the 1990s, around the time when India, coincidentally, had started its globalization process, and everyone knows by now, how Gurgaon has been both its epitome and predicament.

The watermark of commodification has been all over the urban and social space of the city and the production and representation of its postmodern edifices. Afterwards, the whole range of new digital technology and digital culture that followed through the expansion of the web space over the physical and social space marked the information age and Gurgaon transcended through the postmodern to the informational times.

Global networking, connectivity and the exchange of ideas and services in the information era have demanded the need to adopt a technological equilibrium of some sort. Spoken and written languages across the world were different, spaces of operation were located at distant corners of the globe, yet technological similarity bonded them together. The Eurocentric notions of three worlds earlier signified a geo-economic differentiation that has been taken over by the networked society, with the fourth world of the cyberspace hovering over and connecting those so-called worlds. However, such technological connectivity demanded a sophisticated version of it for every player and participant. The information age, indeed, has brought high-technology driven jobs and performance that, on one hand, have increased the quality and income of workers, and on the other, have created socially and economically stratified labour forces with a shrinking middle-class base in a city like Gurgaon.

In terms of spatial disposition, Gurgaon has defied the attempts of any kind of singular entity to control its making. The concept of a master plan and comprehensive planning disappeared here. Neither was a particular logic applied, nor was a specific strategy accepted. In addition to that, no specific time-period was set for developing Gurgaon. Inside the city, one may expect the unexpected—unpredictable juxtapositions of land use and activities, coexistence of the rich and poor, commercial and residential areas. It is a reality that cities cannot be perfect. Any city trying to achieve perfection in a single-shot blueprint has failed miserably, Delhi being one of them. Gurgaon did not have that baggage because it never had any such ideas. The absence of a blueprint usually makes decision-makers and citizens think, negotiate, act and apply corrections to bring back a city on track. During its initial days, Gurgaon did not face much critical resistance in the

Reflection

absence of active citizen groups who could pose questions. By the time residents realized what has been happening, the city was already on its irreversible trajectory.

An interesting way to observe a city is to compare it to a 'collage', especially when its genesis is not guided by a comprehensive plan. Colin Rowe and Fred Koetter, both architects and professors at Yale School of Architecture, famously used collage as an analogy to read the incremental, self-regulating and disjointed nature of cities.[75] Collage, which originates from the French word for 'sticking', is a visual art form prepared by sticking various materials like photographs, pieces of paper and fabric on to a backing surface. It uses pictorial and textual matters from different sources, which are put together to form an underlying meaning. The form is achieved through patchwork with specific significance. This technique can be used to explain the making of Gurgaon, with the limitation that the collage has a conceptual picture to begin with, something that has been missing in Gurgaon. The missing link has further been intensified by the non-related relationships between adjoining parts of the city.

About a decade back, when most of the glittering malls of the NCR were located along MG Road, an architect friend of mine used to call it the Las Vegas of Gurgaon. This moniker has a history. The American architect couple, Robert Venturi and Denise Scott Brown, compiled a book called *Learning from Las Vegas* based on their students' work.[76] The conceptual message of the book received divided opinions, one section appreciated its approach in understanding the postmodern city and the other considered it sacrilegious of established ideas of urbanism. Las Vegas grew after World War II and was considered to be a 'non-city', an outgrown 'strip' fronted by parking lots, gambling casinos, hotels, churches and bars. Gurgaon, too, at the beginning of the millennium was more about the strip along MG Road with its shopping malls. Every year, as Fremont Street in Vegas changed, so did its counterpart in Gurgaon. In both the places, buildings became competitive with adjacent ones, irrespective of whether those were casinos and hotels in Vegas or malls in Gurgaon. Architecture was used to attract attention—buildings, indeed, have been 'decorated sheds' in both places.

In Gurgaon, the collage and strip can be perceived and have contributed to the pattern of its growth. Postmodern cities are expected to have no apparent system of 'overall combination'; instead, they are made by several actors producing patches of local order.[77] In the absence of a High Modern planning document, a contemporary city is built around three broad components: road, node and enclave. The making of Gurgaon supports such a reading.

Here, roads were built first, and many of those were often left incomplete after a certain point. In fact, in the initial stages, developers had problems with the government agencies because the latter spent almost all its money on road-building without investing much on basic services and other infrastructure. Roads worked like 'armature'. At various points on these roads, once buildings were erected,

Reflection

different activities started and nodes were formed. By gaining accessibility via the road, isolated enclaves began to come up. Eventually, a strip was urbanized along the road. Development along Golf Course Road happened exactly in this manner and similar processes preceded and followed it as well.

Despite inconsistencies and contradictions, enclaves, malls, glass offices and villages remained to be parallel realities in Gurgaon. I call this an assortment, and such a city, an 'assorted city'.[78] Gurgaon, like most other contemporary cities, has been constituted by several 'incompatible' spaces. Therefore, such a city has been formed out of heterotopias. The concept of heterotopias is essential to understand the intentions that make the assorted city.

The great French philosopher Michel Foucault introduced the notion of heterotopias in his lecture delivered in French at the French Architecture Research Institute in 1967. The idea became popular much later, when his lecture was published in English around the mid-1980s. Gurgaon's image-building, too, has always attempted to recreate different spaces: Spanish villas, English country house, glass- and aluminium-clad shopping malls, office towers, villages, streetside food vendors—all can be seen to be coexisting on the city palette. These inconsistencies make this type of postmodern city heterotopic in its concepts.

Gurgaon has been a city of multiple players, interconnected by web-like relationships, who made their own urban patch based on certain local reasons. No evident overall coordination can be seen so far. This has been typical of postmodern cities and we are, perhaps, yet to see many settlements of this nature. Most of the enclaves are driven by the desire to be exceptional. Each one of them wants to be different from its adjacent ones or the ones made earlier. Thus, a scattered collection of enclaves with inherent discordance of appearance or the way of living has shaped up, creating the heterotopic city of Gurgaon.

When the government preferred to wash its hands of the meaningful development of the city and utopian and ambitious city-building exercises were long discarded, 'build that sells' became the sole objective of the real estate initiatives. The role of the government in providing necessary urban infrastructure becomes even more essential in this scenario, so that private development can plug and play with it. Judicious urban interventions to improve the city should be adopted by ascertaining urban design and planning guidelines.

POSTSCRIPT

The COVID-19 pandemic has posed new uncertainties about how cities will respond to it eventually. Historically, urban life changed during times of pestilence. With the outbreak of each epidemic, new ways to guide social interaction, address inequities and environmental concerns, as well as to create new occupational roles, took place. The built environment reacted accordingly, over time and across different geographies. How the epidemic will influence social practices and urban services, and what will be its implications on open spaces and public buildings, including schools, workplaces, shopping, will be seen later. Gurgaon, too, may have its own story in store for us to explore in time to come.

※

As I made my way back to Delhi from Gurgaon, late in the afternoon in early winter, I saw vendors slowly winding up their stalls as the huge glass buildings behind them sparkled with lights. Adorned with attractive glow signs, the main roads of Gurgaon always seemed to be in a festive spirit.

An ugly yet effective blue and white street sign thanked me for visiting Gurugram. Gurgaon, I remembered, had been renamed Gurugram in 2016. A city to which history had made very little sense so far, has been presented with a mythological plaque. Will the new name make it a better city? Will it give the city a new identity? Only time will tell.

While I left behind the inscrutable countenance of the city, I looked forward to my next visit, to know the new story of Gurugram.

ACKNOWLEDGEMENTS

Writing about Gurgaon has long been on my agenda. During my active teaching days for 11 years at Sushant School of Art and Architecture in Gurgaon, I had coordinated many design studios and architectural research work on Gurgaon, the first of which was on the redevelopment of MG Road in 2000.

Gurgaon has always been in the making. It is a city continuously changing itself. Like many others, I have been intrigued by the way the city unfolded and took its present shape. My reading of this city has evolved over the years, and my critique of its architecture has remained consistent throughout.

I learned a lot from interacting with my students at Sushant School, who undertook research on and documentation of multiple aspects and areas of the city. My colleagues at the school, too, were very well-informed about the city and some of them continuously reminded me to write about it. Vishal Agarwal was one such colleague and friend who always had an extra bit of information on Gurgaon to share. My former student Amit Madholia, presently in the Town and Country Planning Department in Gurgaon, has been extremely helpful in explaining his thoughts. Jyoti Sagar was willing to offer his refreshing views when he got to know that I was writing on Gurgaon. His wife, Prema, was enthusiastic about sharing her part of the story as well. Latika Thukral's observations were highly informative. Pramod Bhasin's views were very thought-provoking. The principal of the senior secondary school in old Gurgaon was cordial and Dr Rajendra Yadav, one of her former colleagues in the school, shared valuable information as well.

Rupa Publications has extended its support right from the beginning. The team patiently coordinated its publication and did a meticulous editing job.

Vina, my wife, has been very supportive of this endeavour. So has been Subhadip, my younger brother. My son, Devneil, has observed the progress of my work quietly and gave his opinions when those were sought.

NOTES

1. Sundaram, Ravi. (2010) *Pirate Modernity: Delhi's media urbanism*. Routledge, New Delhi
2. Rangnekar, D.K. (1964) Nehruism and the Second Phase. *The Economic Weekly*. Special Number Vol. 16, Issue No. 29–30–31, 18 July
3. Among them, 93 per cent were owners or their dependents and the remaining 7 per cent tenants were ex-proprietors who lost their land because of poverty, misbehaviour or lack of skill.
4. Gurgaon District Gazetteer (1983) Chapter IV on 'Agriculture and Irrigation', p. 144
5. Ibid.
6. Barnes, Tim. 'Informal Labour in Urban India: Three Cities, Three Journeys'. In: Michael Gillan, Michael & Lambert, Rob (Eds.) (2015) *India and the Age of Crisis: The Local Politics of Global Economic and Ecological Fragility*. Routledge, Oxon, UK
7. Central Ground Water Board (August 2015) 'Report on Aquifer Mapping and Management Plan', National Capital Region (NCR), Haryana, Volume-I, Ministry of Water Resources, River Development and Ganga Rejuvenation, Government of India, North Western Region, Chandigarh, pp. 9–11
8. Gurgaon District Gazetteer (1910) mentioned that in some wells in Rewari, a different kind of water was found, known as 'matwala', or hard, the crops of which were generally good. As per Gurgaon District Gazetteer (1983), an analysis of 1,914 water

samples taken from 518 villages prior to the reorganization of the district in 1972 indicated that on an average, 30 per cent of the villages in the district had good, 28 per cent marginal and 33 per cent poor quality underground water.

9   Economic and Statistical Organization (1971) 'Gurgaon Canal Project—An Evaluation Study'. Publication No. 73. Planning Department, Government of Haryana

10 Gurgaon Canal was a 'perennial canal' planned to utilize the capacity in the Bhakra canals and provide irrigation to Gurgaon district from Ravi-Beas water for 265 days in a year. For the remaining 100 days in the monsoon period, water from Yamuna River would be taken. The project started in 1960–61, but was suspended in 1962 due to the Indo-China War. The work resumed in April 1964 to be completed as per the revised schedule in 1967–68. However, the canal could not be opened for regular operation in 1968–69 and was completed by June 1972.
    From: Economic and Statistical Organization (1971). 'Gurgaon Canal Project—An Evaluation Study'. Publication No. 73. Planning Department, Government of Haryana

11 Central Water Commission Inter State Matters Directorate (2015) *Legal Instruments on Rivers in India (Vol–III): Agreements on Inter State Rivers, Part One*. October, pp. 137–139 [Online] http://www.cwc.gov.in/sites/default/files/legalinst-Vol-III(Part1).pdf [Accessed October 27, 2020]

12 Debroy, Bibek & Bhandari, Laveesh. (September 2009) 'Gurgaon and Faridabad—An Exercise in Contrasts'. *CDDRL Working Paper No. 101*. Centre on Democracy, Development and The Rule of Law, Stanford University

13 Gurunani, Shubhra. (2013) 'Flexible Planning: The making of India's Millennium City, Gurgaon'. In: Redemacher, Anna & Sivaramakrishnan, K. (eds.) 2013. *Ecologies of Urbanism in India: Metropolitan Civility and Sustainability*. Hong Kong University

14 Singh, K.P. (2015 [2011]). *Whatever the Odds: the incredible story behind DLF.* Harper Collins India, Delhi. p. 98
15 U/s 4 (1) of the Punjab Scheduled Roads and Controlled Areas Restriction of Unregulated Development Act, 1963
16 For controlled area maps: TCPO Website https://tcpharyana.gov.in/ControlledArea/Gurgaon/Plans/1%20Gurgaon%20CA-I.pdf> [Accessed April 2, 2017]
17 Gurunani, Shubhra. (2013). 'Flexible Planning: The making of India's Millennium City, Gurgaon'. In: Redemacher, Anna & Sivaramakrishnan, K. (eds.) 2013. *Ecologies of Urbanism in India: Metropolitan Civility and Sustainability.* Hong Kong University Press, Hong Kong. pp. 119–143
18 Provisions were inserted in u/s 7(1) of the Punjab Scheduled Roads and Controlled Areas Restriction of Unregulated Development Act, 1963 and new sub-section of 7A was created, both by Haryana Act 16 of 1996
19 Nallathiga, R. (2009) Potential of Land and Land-based Instruments for Infrastructure Development in Urban Areas. *India Infrastructure Report 2009: Land – a critical resource for infrastructure.* 3i Network, Infrastructure Development Finance Company. Oxford University Press, New Delhi, pp. 218–226

Gill, H.S. (2002) *Policies and Projects for Land and Shelter Development for Delhi—Implementation Mechanisms,* Human Settlements Management Institute, Delhi.
20 U/s 3(1) of the Act, to obtain a licence to develop a colony, an owner shall have to make an application to the Director, TCPO, along with prescribed fees, conversion charges, and the income-tax clearance certificate. However, the Director may grant exemption (u/s 9(1) of the Act) to a person from obtaining the licence if he is satisfied that:

'the land (i) had been divided into plots and more than 20 per cent of the plots according to layout plan; (ii) is in a compact block; and (iii) is not situated within the controlled area; or (i) the land does not exceed 4,000 square metres and is situated within the limits of a municipal area/a notified area or the Faridabad complex; (ii) the amenities similar to the one existing in the locality exit or such person undertakes to provide such amenities; and (iii) the size of the plots divided or proposed to be divided is in conformity with the general layout of the plots in the locality.'

21 Letter No. 8DP-88/12105–12705, dated 14/21.11.80 on the Subject: Selection of sites and acquisition of land by Government department/Corporate Bodies etc. [Online] https://tcpharyana.gov.in/Policy/CDoc1.pdf [Accessed 27 October, 2017]

22 Nallathiga, R. (2009) Potential of Land and Land-based Instruments for Infrastructure Development in Urban Areas. *India Infrastructure Report 2009: Land – a critical resource for infrastructure*. 3i Network, Infrastructure Development Finance Company. Oxford University Press, New Delhi, pp. 218–226

Joardar, S.D. (2007) Land development Mechanisms in building the City: Gurgaon vis-à-vis Delhi. *Dialogues*, Sushant School of Art and Architecture, Gurgaon. pp. 25– 27

23 Eleven states where ULCRA was introduced were: Andhra Pradesh, Gujarat, Haryana, Himachal Pradesh, Karnataka, Maharashtra, Orissa, Punjab, Tripura, Uttar Pradesh and West Bengal, and all the Union Territories

Acharya, Ballabh Prasad. (1989) *The Indian Urban Land Ceiling Act: A Critique of the 1976 Legislation*, Asian Institute of Technology, Thailand, The World Bank

24 Ved Pal vs. State of Haryana and others on 18 November, 2011 (CWP Nos.17208, 17292, 16755, 16760, 16807 & 17217of 2010) in the High Court of Punjab and Haryana at Chandigarh (at the room of Hon'ble Justice Satish Kumar Mittal and Hon'ble Justice Paramjeet Singh). https://indiankanoon.org/

doc/60851158/?type=print [Accessed 10 April 2017]
25 Ibid.
26 Behl, Abhishek. (2016) 'High cost of land acquisition slows down new Huda projects in Gurgaon'. The Hindustan Times. Sept 23. [Online] http://www.hindustantimes.com/gurgaon/high-cost-of-land-acquisition-slows-down-new-huda-projects-in-gurgaon/story-fxCM9Zz6I8LBVXena2RjHL.html [Accessed 27 April 2017]
27 Ibid.
28 Gill, H.S. (2002) *Policies and Projects for Land and Shelter Development for Delhi—Implementation Mechanisms.* Human Settlements Management Institute, Delhi.
Reprinted in: 3iNetwork (2009) *Land-A Critical Resource for Infrastructure.* India Infrastructure Report. Infrastructure Development Finance Company, New Delhi
29 Singh, K.P. (2015[2011]). *Whatever the Odds: The incredible story behind DLF.* Harper Collins India, Delhi. p. 107
30 Nayar, Kuldip. (2016 [1977]) *Emergency Retold.* Konark Publishers Pvt. Ltd, New Delhi (First Published as *The Judgement* in 1977)
Mehta, Vinod. (2015[1978]) *The Sanjay Story.* HarperCollins Publishers India, Noida
Besides above two, Maruti Suzuki's current chairman, R.C. Bhargava's book was also a good source of information: Bhargava R.C. and Seetha. (2010) *The Maruti Story: How a Public Sector Company put India on Wheels*, Collins Business: An Imprint of HarperCollins Publishers, Noida.
31 Mehta, Vinod. (2015[1978]) *The Sanjay Story.* HarperCollins Publishers India, Noida, p. 78
32 Bhargava R.C. and Seetha. (2010) *The Maruti Story: How a Public Sector Company put India on Wheels*, Collins Business: An Imprint of HarperCollins Publishers, Noida.
33 Gill, H.S. (2002) *Policies and Projects for Land and Shelter Development for Delhi—Implementation Mechanisms,* Human Settlements

Management Institute, Delhi.
34 Sehran, Sohail and Sinha, Snehil. (Dec 19, 2015) 'Gurgaon's Galleria is 3rd costliest market in India: Report'. [Online] *The Hindustan Times*.http://www.hindustantimes.com/gurgaon/galleria-is-3rd-costliest-market-in-india/story-m6LXK3OT4zV0KE03Z5pHsO.html [Accessed Nov 20, 2017]
In its annual report titled 'Main Streets Across the World', the real estate firm Cushman and Wakefield discussed that markets in Delhi-NCR have seen a constant rise in rentals over the years and suggested that the average monthly rental rate in Galleria is about 750 per sq. ft. (in 2015).
35 Singh, K.P. (2015[2011]) *Whatever the Odds: The Incredible Story Behind DLF*. Harper Collins India, Delhi. p. 215–230
36 Chatterji, Tathagata. (2015) *Citadels of Glass: The Story of India's New Suburban Landscape*. Westland Ltd., Chennai, p. 73.
37 Ibid.
38 LiveMint (Dec 03, 2014) How Gurgaon was built, licence by licence, govt by govt: An interactive graphic on land allotments to developers in the last 34 years. *LiveMint E paper* [online] http://www.livemint.com/Companies/rkUwUVtzAflBP7hPVa1roL/How-Gurgaon-was-built-licence-by-licence-government-by-gov.html [Accessed Nov 20, 2017]
39 Town and Country Planning Department (Nov 15, 2012) *Haryana Government Gazetteer.* Government of Haryana
40 Yardley, Jim. (June 9, 2011) 'The Gurgaon story: A mirror to India's growth.' [Online] http://www.ndtv.com/gurgaonnews/thegurgaonstoryamirrortoin diasgrowth458043 [Accessed June 6 2017]
Also, Yardley, Jim. (June 8, 2011) 'In India, dynamism wrestles with dysfunction.' Asia Pacific Section, *New York Times*
41 Ibid.
42 Srivatsava, Sanjay. (2015) *Entangled Urbanism: Slum, Gated*

Notes

Community, and Shopping Mall in Delhi and Gurgaon. Oxford University Press, New Delhi

43 Kumar, Rakesh (n.d) 'Ground Water Conditions and Water Conservation done by Agriculture Department in Haryana State,' Department of Agriculture and Farmers Welfare, Government of Haryana [Online] http://jalshakti-dowr.gov.in/sites/default/files/WaterConservation-Haryana.pdf [Accessed 20 Oct, 2020]. This is based on a presentation made by Kumar, chief hydrologist in the Ground Water Cell of the department. Besides that, there are a number of research papers, for example, Sitender and Rajeshwari (2015) 'Estimation of Ground Water Resource of Gurgaon District, Haryana'. *Journal of Land use and Water Management*, Volume 14, Issue 1, pp. 26–36 or, newspaper reports on this issue, see for example: Arora-Desai, Prayag. (Apr 06, 2019) 'Gurugram water table falls 3 metres in 5 years, extraction at 308%', *The Hindustan Times* [Online] https://www.hindustantimes.com/gurgaon/gurugram-water-table-falls-3-metres-in-5-years-extraction-at-308/story-LkX4eLsrlmUYT24DAyn1zO.html [Accessed 10 September 2020]

44 Sharma, Manoj. (Sep 24, 2017) 'Writers' muse: The dark, mysterious, fascinating, funny tales from Gurgaon'. *The Hindustan Times,* Gurgaon [Online] http://www.hindustantimes.com/gurgaon/tales-from-gurgaon-dark-and-mysterious-and-fascinating/story-TKyLn1wLRtI4Ykk727RpFP.html [Accessed 16 Oct, 2017]

45 Hafeez Contractor Architects. [Online Page in the ebuild.in Portal]. https://ebuild.in/dlf-gateway-tower-gurgaon. [Accessed 18 August, 2017]

46 Malhotra, Shriya. (July 2013) Gurgaon's Gateway Tower: A Symbol of Unsustainability. [online webpage:] Failed Architecture. https://www.failedarchitecture.com/gurgaons-gateway-tower-a-symbol-of-unsustainability/ [Accessed 18 August, 2017]

47 Debord, Guy. (1994[1967]) *The Society of the Spectacles*. Translation by: Donald Nicholson-Smith. Zone Books, New York (Originally in French published in 1967 by Buchet Chastel, France).
48 Lynch, Kevin. (1960) *The Image of the City*. Cambridge MA: MIT Press.
   Lynch went on to highlight these five visual elements as:
   Districts: areas having common visual characteristics (not administrative districts)
   Landmarks: easily identifiable and visible physical objects in the urban landscape
   Nodes: spaces guiding the direction in a city, like squares, plazas, parks
   Edges: road-edges, boundaries of two different areas—an indication of break in the contiguity
   Paths: routes, roads, footpaths along which people move in the city
49 *Indian Express Sunday Magazine,* December 8, 2002
   Quoted in: Sengupta, Ranjana. (2007) *Delhi Metropolitan: The making of an unlikely city*. Penguin Books India, Gurgaon, p. 158
50 Jameson, Fredric. (1998[2009]) *The Cultural Turn: Selected Writings on the Postmodern 1983–1998*. Verso, London, New York
51 Ibid. p. 4
52 Ibid. p 111
53 Biswas, Suptendu P. (2007) 'Gurgaon: An Isolated Urbanism'. *Dialogues*, Proceedings of a symposium on the shaping of Gurgaon, Sushant School of Art & Architecture. Gurgaon. p. 10
54 Times News Network. (Oct 11, 2017) *The Times of India*. [online] https://timesofindia.indiatimes.com/city/gurgaon/govt-raises-cap-from-10-to-15-acres-per-sector-for-affordable-homes/articleshow/61028467.cms [Accessed 18 Oct 2017]
   Ahuja, Sanjeev K. (Jun 11, 2016) 36,000 affordable housing units on offer in Gurgaon. *The Hindustan Times*. Gurgaon [Online] http://

www.hindustantimes.com/gurgaon/36-000-affordable-housing-units-on-offer-in-gurgaon/story-THkcGjlaQId5owXtEh4V9H.html [Accessed 20 Oct 2017]

55 Times News Network. (TNN) (Mar 14, 2016) For 150 years, a guardian of faith. *The Times of India*. Gurgaon [Online] https://timesofindia.indiatimes.com/city/gurgaon/For-150-years-a-guardian-of-faith/articleshow/51386680.cms [Accessed 21 Oct 2017]

56 Raj, Amrit. (Aug 7, 2012) 'Maruti to build low-cost houses for workers in Haryana, Gujarat'. *The Mint*. [Online] http://www.livemint.com/Companies/ngVbLK1uPVEPbiDBa4kfPM/Maruti-to-build-lowcost-houses-for-workers-in-Haryana-Guja.html [Accessed 26 May 2017]

57 Castells, Manuel. (1989) *The Informational City: Information Technology, Economic Restructuring and the Urban-Regional Process*. Blackwell Publishers, Oxford and Cambridge, p. 218

58 Dayal, Sakshi. (Aug 17, 2016) 'As Dalits start winning, 'friendly' kabaddi match turns violent in Gurgaon'. *The Indian Express*. Gurgaon Edition. [Online] http://indianexpress.com/article/india/india-news-india/gurgaon-dalit-kabaddi-match-violence-yadav-2979903/ [Accessed May 25, 2017]

59 Sandhu, Veenu. (Feb 2, 2013) 'The great divide'. *Business Standard*, New Delhi. [Online] http://www.business-standard.com/article/beyond-business/the-great-divide-113020200078_1.html[Accessed May 20, 2017]

60 In 2013, the Juvenile Justice Board sentenced Akash Yadav for the murder of his classmate, Abhishek Tyagi, in 2007. Yadav brought his father's gun, hidden in a sock, to school. The boys had been quarreling for several days, and on the fateful day, Yadav and one of his friends confronted Tyagi in the campus after school hours and shot him from close range.

Sengupta, Somini. (Dec 12, 2007) 'In India, a Rare School

Shooting Leaves 14–Year-Old Dead'. *The New York Times.* [Online] http://www.nytimes.com/2007/12/12/world/asia/12india.html [Accessed June 1, 2017]

Post Script: Yadav was once again wanted when he allegedly shot his friend five times after an argument in Gurgaon in March 2015.

61 VSPB Associates. (2017) Revitalisation of derelict urban spaces: *Bundh* rejuvenation and eco-restoration of urban forest, Gurugram. *Journal of Landscape Architecture.* No. 51, pp. 70–75 (Text by Vina Verghese Biswas)

62 Bhasin, Tanushree. (May 11, 2013) 'The real estate boom has jeopardised NCR forests'. *The Sunday Guardian.* [Online} http://www.sunday-guardian.com/young-restless/the-real-estate-boom-has-jeopardised-ncr-forests. [Accessed 09 December 2017]

63 Agarwal, Chetan. (2017) 'Who owns, who zones, Mangar Bani?' In: Pande, Alka (eds.) *Land Art.* Visual Art Gallery, India Habitat Centre, pp. 70–79

64 Ibid.

65 iamgurgaon website. [Online] http://iamgurgaon.org/aravalli-biodiversity-park/ [Accessed December 2, 2017]

66 See for example the chapter titled, 'The High-Modernist City: An experiment and a critique' (pp.103–146) in: Scott, James C (1998) *Seeing like a state: How certain schemes to improve the human condition have failed.* Yale University Press, New Haven and London.

67 Biswas, Suptendu P. (2015) *Assorted City: Equity, justice and politics in urban services delivery.* Sage, New Delhi, p. 41

68 Ibid. p.131.

69 Times News Network (Feb 22, 2017) 'Mumbai India's richest city, 2 Kolkata localities among most affluent': New World Wealth report. *The Times of India.* [Online] https://timesofindia.indiatimes.com/india/mumbai-indias-richest-city-2-kolkata-localities-among-most-affluent-new-world-wealth-report/articleshow/57273267.cms [Accessed 10 December 2017]

70 Kumar, Kartik. (Aug 14, 2017) 'Gurgaon: Agreement signed for reviving defunct Bandhwari waste plant'. *The Hindustan Times*. [Online] http://www.hindustantimes.com/gurgaon/gurgaon-agreement-signed-for-reviving-defunct-bandhwari-waste-plant/story-f6uc3k4scKnj6zzYgiyEHP.html [Accessed 20 November 2017]

71 Dhankar, Leena. (October 26, 2016) 'Gurgaon: Magnolias goes eco-friendly, sets up waste treatment plant'. *The Hindustan Times*. [Online] http://www.hindustantimes.com/gurgaon/gurgaon-magnolias-goes-eco-friendly-sets-up-waste-treatment-plant/story-0iupoozCG0q0MKqOqe7lcM.html [Accessed 20 November 2017]

72 Ibid.

73 Ibid.

74 Jameson, Fredric. (1998[2009]) *The Cultural Turn: Selected Writings on the Postmodern 1983–1998*. Verso, London, New York

75 Rowe, Colin and Koetter, Fred. (1978) *Collage City*. MIT Press, Cambridge: MA

76 Venturi, Robert, Scott Brown, Denise and Izenour, Steven. (1977[1972]) *Learning from Las Vegas*. MIT Press, Cambridge, MA
The husband-wife architect team of Venturi and Scott Brown, assisted by Steven Izenour, guided a group of post-grad architecture students to urban form at Las Vegas at Yale School of Art and Architecture. The module was called 'Learning from Las Vegas' and the students' research work was later converted into the book.

77 Shane, David Grahame. (2005) *Recombinant Urbanism: Conceptual Modelling in Architecture, Urban Design and City Theory*. John Wiley & Sons Ltd. Chichester, England
More germane to this discussion is the commentary of David Grahame Shane, a faculty member in the Urban Design programme at Columbia University. In this book, he has given an exhaustive account historical and theoretical account of postmodern cities.

He recognizes three elements of contemporary urbanism: enclave, armature and heterotopias. However, his discussions are more technical in nature revolving around notions of urban design and city reading.

78 Biswas, Suptendu P. (2015) *Assorted City: Equity, Justice and Politics in Urban Services Delivery*. Sage, New Delhi
Previously, I have discussed this phenomenon in details in my first book that looked at water supply as urban basic services to read the 'equity mosaics' in the city.

Made in the USA
Monee, IL
03 May 2026